5 Steps to Successful Home Schooling

How to Add Faith and Focus to Your Home Education Program

By Pamela Patnode

Philomena Press
Minneapolis

Copyright © 2012 Pamela Patnode

Nihil Obstat: Rev. George Welzbacher. Censor Librorum. April 3, 2012

Imprimatur: + Most Reverend John C. Nienstedt, Archbishop of St. Paul and Minneapolis. April 4, 2012

No part of this work may be reproduced or transmitted in any form or by any means, electronic or mechanical, including photocopying and recording, or by any information storage or retrieval system without the prior written consent of the copyright owner. Requests to publisher for permission should be addressed to the Permission Department at Philomena Press.

Philomena Press LLC
6569 Garland Lane N.
Minneapolis, MN 55311

All Bible quotations and citations come from the Catholic Study Bible: New American Bible.

ISBN: 978-0-615-62947-6

For Dan, Jeff, Claire, Kristen, Katie and Grace.

And for Fr. Arnold.

TABLE OF CONTENTS

Acknowledgments..v

Foreword by Fr. Arnold Weber, OSB.. vii

Introduction..1

Step 1: Pray..5

Step 2: Establish Your Mission..27

Step 3: Read Quality Literature..47

Step 4: Get Organized..67

Step 5: Find Support..85

Bonus Section: How to Begin Home Schooling Quickly............111

Conclusion..123

Appendix A: How to Pray the Rosary..125

Appendix B: Curriculum Providers and Other Resources............129

Appendix C: Sample Daily Home School Schedules....................147

Bibliography..151

Acknowledgments

This book would not be in print were it not for the help, support, and encouragement of numerous people. *First and foremost, I thank my husband.* He has been my champion and helpmate throughout the process. Not only is he my right hand man with the publication of this book, but also with home schooling and family life. *In addition, I thank my children.* Each of them provided enthusiasm from start to finish, which kept me motivated, even through difficult times. They have also been my students, "guinea pigs", and champions throughout this journey we call home schooling.

Fr. Arnold Weber, OSB carefully reviewed the book with the eyes of an educator and theologian. He also wrote the foreword for the book, and offered support and encouragement throughout the process. Fr. Arnold passed away shortly before the book went to press. I miss him dearly.

Laurie Swing offered her professional editing services. Her thoughtful, word by word scrutiny and recommendations improved the manuscript greatly. I am truly appreciative of her help.

Laurie Anderson, Janet Bezdicek, and *Sunny Scott* read through the manuscript to offer recommended enhancements and their ringing endorsements. To all of them, I am forever grateful.

Emily Cavins provided publishing knowledge that proved to be of tremendous value. Her help is much appreciated.

To all of the women of the *Plymouth/Wayzata Home School Group, Class Act Theatre Group,* and the *Friday Morning St. Anne's Group,* I thank you for your beautiful Christian witness. You have been my role models, mentors, and friends. Thank you for being my companions on this home education journey.

Finally, *Laura Spaeth* used her creative genius to take my simple text document and transform it into this beautifully designed book. I am both grateful to her and in awe of her talent.

FOREWORD

By: Fr. Arnold Weber, OSB

The last 25 years has seen many educational changes, some of which have been disappointing. Because of the problems in both public education and, sadly, even Catholic education, parents have looked for different educational options. About twenty-five years ago, I became acquainted with home schooling. At that time, I had some misgivings about this educational method. I wondered, "Will they miss out on what our culture has to offer? Will they be properly socialized? Can they participate in extra-curricular activities?" Over the years, I observed as a number of my parishioners home educated their children, including the author of this book. I have seen that none of my concerns were realized. In fact, I saw the opposite. However, I still wondered what resources were available for the Catholic home schooling family to help them succeed in their efforts. Now I see a marvelous resource – Pamela Patnode's book *5 Steps to Successful Home Schooling*. This book is tremendously helpful, not only for Catholic home school families. The aims of the program are sound. This manual is practical, has good content, and is very instructive. I'm 85 years old with many years of religious participation, and I found the manual challenging, good doctrine, and viable methods. I am pleased to submit my endorsement of this book to you. - Fr. Arnold Weber, OSB

Fr. Arnold Weber, OSB (1925-2012) was a Roman Catholic priest and Benedictine monk at St. John's Abbey and University, Collegeville, MN. For most of his sixty years as an ordained priest, Fr. Weber worked in the areas of education and pastoral life. Indeed, Fr. Weber had vast experience in the area of education serving as teacher, principal, president, and chairman of Catholic high schools, prep schools, elementary schools, and religious education programs within the Twin Cities and outlying areas. His final pastoral assignment was pastor of a parish of 2,800 families in the Minneapolis area with a parochial school of 400 (and 1,200 in the religious education program). Fr. Weber served as pastor of this parish for 23 years. He had a very practical experience with family life and education, and was witness to a great number of changes in both areas. Fr. Weber passed away shortly before this book went to press.

Introduction

A few years ago, my friend Kathy called to ask how she could get started with home schooling. Their son, an athletic, handsome, intelligent young man was being bullied. As the problem escalated, and all attempts with the school and the perpetrator failed, the family decided to pull their child from the school and educate him at home. My friend needed information, resources, and support, and she needed it quickly. There was so much I wanted to share with her, so much I wanted to pass along. However, because of her unique situation, and the urgency she felt, I knew I needed to boil down all the information I had into a few manageable and focused steps to help them get started. Later that year, I had two other friends call me to ask about home schooling. Their situations were not as urgent because they were making plans for the following school year. They, too, asked for my help.

Any veteran home schooler who has received a call like this can understand how difficult it is to succinctly provide the information needed to help someone begin. There is just so much to share! There is information on the benefits of home schooling and how to gain these blessings. There are educational philosophies that are valuable to read about and, in some cases, adopt. There are excellent curriculum resources to discuss, great literature to share, support groups worth joining, paper work to complete, conferences to attend, articles to read, etc., etc., etc.!

What I've learned from home schooling my children is that it is important to have a specific road map - a well thought out plan - in place. *5 Steps to Successful Home Schooling* will help you prepare this plan. This book will help you design a blueprint for your child's education, guide you on how to put this plan into action, and assure you that home schooling will not jeopardize the academic or social development of your child. Indeed, successful home schooling can bring about *excellence* – excellence in academics as well as excellence in character development. In many cases it takes a leap of faith to begin home schooling, but it is well worth the jump!

Little did I know back when I received that first phone call asking for help, that it would be the beginning of this book. Trying to offer help to my friends forced me to begin thinking about the important steps we need to take to successfully home educate our children. Receiving these phone calls surprised me for a number of reasons. First, because I still do not consider myself an 'expert' on this topic. Each year brings about new challenges, and I am continually reading new books, attending conferences, and asking my friends for advice. Second, the *number* of calls I have received throughout the years surprises me. And yet, these calls are a reflection of the current growth of the home schooling movement.

In 1989, while a student at the University of Wisconsin – Madison, I met a young man who mentioned that he had been home schooled. He was the first person I had ever met who had been home educated. Educating at home was rare twenty to thirty years ago. Today, however, the home schooling movement has taken off. In 2010, the number of home educated youth topped 2 million school age students. This is equivalent to one in every twenty-five children (HSLDA 2011).

The reasons people have for choosing to home educate their children are many and varied, but their reasons have led to rapid and tremendous growth. Because of this extensive growth in home schooling, the resources available to those who home educate are staggering. Whereas the 'pioneers' of the home schooling movement were forced to search far and wide (often under the fear of legal repercussion) for curriculum materials, social networks, and support; today's home educators are bombarded with materials, co-ops, classes, field trip opportunities, clubs, and social networks. Making sense of the myriad of choices can be intimidating and frightening. I know because I was there. In fact, I still am. Each year brings new challenges and goals and I find myself trying to discern which of all the offerings available will be of greatest benefit to my children and my family as a whole. Fortunately, throughout my years as a home educator, I have learned some valuable lessons that have improved our home schooling experience. I have also been tremendously blessed by the wisdom and experience of many home schooling mothers in our area. Over the years, these wise women have shared many insights with me that have proven to be invaluable. It is the combination of my own experience and the wisdom of others that I now share with you.

My own home schooling experience has been extremely positive. Prior to home educating, our three older children were enrolled in a Catholic school where they had a beautiful experience with excellent teachers and wonderful friends. When we first sent our son off to kindergarten, I never imagined that we would be home schooling four years later. But, God is good, and He had different plans for our family. He placed upon my heart a genuine curiosity about home schooling, and put people in my path who home educated their children. Finally, although I volunteered for many programs and activities within the school, *God helped me realize that I was involved with my children's school without being involved with my children.* God was calling me to focus more on my family and His will for us. With one child in third grade and two others in first grade and kindergarten, I researched home education. I met with people I knew who home schooled, attended home schooling conferences, read as many books on the topic as I could get my hands on, and prayed. My husband and I said we'd give it a year. If it was a total disaster, we'd re-enroll the kids after the first semester.

3

Many years later, we find ourselves still home schooling. It has been a tremendous blessing to our family, and we have shared memories together that will last a lifetime. Indeed, the single greatest blessing from our home schooling experience is *the quality time I have spent with the people who mean the absolute most to me*, namely my husband and my children. It has blessed me beyond measure to have spent, and continue to spend, hour upon hour each and every day with one another. We have read books aloud (laughing and crying together), we have enjoyed field trips, drama productions, and family vacations that tie in with what we're learning in history, science, or geography. We've struggled through fractions, learned our phonograms, made a history timeline that begins with creation and runs through to the present day (It took us five years to cover that much history!), and most of all, we've loved. We have learned to love each other, even when we're not at our best, and we've learned to love learning.

In addition to building strong family relationships, my children have been successful in the areas of academics, social relationships, athletics, and their faith development. Through careful prayer, planning, and perseverance, we have found a system that allows each child to define and then reach their potential. Whether you are new to home schooling, or have been home educating for a while, I hope that the steps in this book will bless your family. Although each child is unique, as is the family from which they come, following these steps will lead to greater success by offering you direction and focus on your journey. What are these five steps?

The five steps to successful home schooling are, in proper order:

1. Pray!
2. Establish your mission
3. Read quality literature
4. Get organized
5. Find support

STEP 1: PRAY!

He was praying in a certain place, and when he had finished, one of his disciples said to him, "Lord, teach us to pray just as John taught his disciples." (Luke 11:1)

When was the last time you paused to consider the tremendous gift of your children? To be a parent is such a blessing. I can think of no job more valuable . . . or more challenging. These days, raising honest, hard working, respectful children into adults with faith and integrity is more difficult than ever. It probably comes as no surprise to you that, in today's culture, the traditional, Christian family is under attack. As a Catholic home schooling parent, you are definitely counter-cultural! Many will look at you with raised eyebrows. Others will voice their skepticism. "What about high school chemistry?" they will ask. "What about sports?" "What about socialization?"

Our culture programs whoever will listen to demand *instant gratification* in all its forms . . . nobody must be made to wait for anything. It also elevates *parenting experts* to a towering level of superiority. But who are these 'parenting experts'? Usually, they are school personnel, doctors, coaches, magazine editors, TV personalities, or even the government. Rarely does this exalted group include a child's own parents. So, if you decide to home educate your child - thereby *delaying personal goals* and *claiming yourself as the expert* on the needs of your own children - you are taking a radical step that will confuse many and anger some. By swimming against the cultural current, you will need to stand firm in your convictions and face down the skeptics you encounter.

Along with defending your decision to home school, of course, you also must educate your child! You will need to select math and reading programs, and history and science curricula that work for your children - and then actually complete them. How can you do it all when the odds seem to be stacked so high against you?

The answer is prayer. Yes, the single most important step in any home school program - the step that can most guarantee blessing is prayer . . . regular and continuous daily prayer.

Our culture is one of great haste. Everyone is in a hurry. Americans are great at doing many things. People are not as good, however, at pondering many things. Prayer forces you to ponder, and before you rush into something as important as the education of your children, take time to ponder and pray. God, alone, knows your innermost needs and those of your spouse, children, and family as a whole. He has wonderful plans for you, but you must communicate regularly with Him if you hope to know those plans.

Most Christians believe, to some degree, that prayer is important. Many of us can recite a handful of prayers by memory. Some of us pray before and after meals, at bedtime, or with our children before they go to sleep. This is a good start, but let me forewarn you. Home schooling your children will likely bring you to your knees more often than few other things in life. Patience, humility, grace, wisdom, and fortitude will be required in measures you may not have experienced up until now. And that's just on the first day of school! The second day will require more of the same, along with some creativity, spontaneity, and humor thrown in for good measure. By the time you reach the first weekend, thoroughly exhausted, your level of virtue will be tested even more when friends, family, and

STEP 1: PRAY

even strangers offer their sarcastic comments, curious questions, and 'helpful' suggestions. Then, week two will begin!

Is this a dismal picture of home schooling? Without prayer, it can be. Few of us by nature possess the saintly amount of virtue required for this job. However, because our God is so good, so generous, and so loving, the necessary doses of virtue are there for the taking. We simply need to ask.

For those of you just beginning to home school, don't let my warnings scare you away from the task. Home schooling your child may seem like a difficult, even scary decision to make. Be encouraged! With God's help, you can achieve success, and reap many blessings along the way.

For those of you who have been home educating for a number of years, the earlier warnings are no surprise to you. As I mentioned earlier, home schooling has been a blessing for our family. It has caused us to grow closer in ways I couldn't have imagined at the outset. This wonderful blessing, however, has come as the result of many, many hours of prayer. On our home school journey, we've encountered difficult days and difficult people. In addition, some lessons have been fun and exciting, while others were arduous and challenging. Yet, with prayer, effort, and perseverance, we continue to follow God's lead on this wonderful adventure in home schooling.

Without question, prayer is the most important step to a successful home schooling experience. *So, how should you pray?* Well, the prayer life of each individual is unique. However, it might be helpful to look at what Christ, our best role model, teaches about prayer. In looking at His prayer life, we see that 1) Jesus prayed alone and He prayed with others; 2) He prayed *before* He started anything; and 3) He prayed often.

7

5 Steps to Successful Home Schooling

Pray Alone...

We know that Jesus prayed often and He prayed with great intensity. The disciples noticed this, too. Furthermore, they noticed that Jesus was energized through prayer. They desired this transformation in their lives so they asked Jesus to teach them to pray. If we look closely at what He taught the disciples, we, too, can learn to pray. In Matthew's gospel, the first thing Jesus did following His baptism was go out into the desert alone. He fasted for forty days before being tempted by the devil. How interesting it is that, before beginning His ministry, He spent time alone in prayer. He did not race out into the streets preaching and healing. No, He began His work by first spending time in private prayer (Matthew 4:1-11).

Upon returning from the desert, Jesus instructed His disciples on how to pray. He told them to go to an inner room and close the door where they could pray in private (Matthew 6:5-15). Praying alone was necessary for Christ, and it is necessary for us, too. As a home schooling parent, you need to spend time alone with God, sharing your joys, fears, successes, and failures. You must remember that He is in control and continually ask for the wisdom to know His will and the grace to do it well.

How to pray

How *you* pray in private might be different from how your friend prays. Private prayer is your special time alone with God. How you spend that time will be unique to your relationship with Him. Many of us desire to grow in our prayer life, but find it difficult to know how to begin. Learning about different forms of prayer, and then trying some of them, can be a starting place. Some methods of private prayer that people throughout the centuries have found beneficial to their spiritual growth are listed below. Those listed

STEP 1: PRAY

on the following pages include praying with the Bible, rote prayer, spontaneous prayer, and adoration. It would be worth trying all of these methods. You might find one form of prayer to be more meaningful than another. Some people find that having variety in their prayer life adds vitality to their spiritual journey. Other people prefer one or two prayer forms and enjoy the rhythm, repetition, and contemplation that this offers. Try them all and see which ones work best for you!

Biblical Prayer

The Bible is God's most holy word, often referred to as His love letter to us. St. Jerome said that "ignorance of Scripture is ignorance of Christ." Indeed, to deepen your relationship with Christ, knowledge of the Word of God is a must. To use Scripture as prayer, however, you need to distinguish Bible study from Bible prayer.

Bible study is the practice of studying the Bible under the learned direction of a Bible scholar. Such studies are held at most churches. There are also excellent Bible study programs available on-line and at many Christian retail outlets. Participation in Bible studies can be of incalculable value and is strongly encouraged by the Church (CCC 110-119). Without question, it has increased my understanding of the Bible, increased my faith, enriched my prayer life, and strengthened my relationship with Christ. However, Bible study is not the same as prayer, although the two go hand in hand. Studying the Bible tends to be an intellectual process. Praying is a contemplative exercise.

There are many different ways to pray with the Bible. Some people enjoy reading and meditating on the Psalms while others read through different books of the Bible, pausing to reflect upon certain verses they encounter. Still others will use a devotional as an aid to their Scripture-based prayer. They read the Bible passages designated for each day and then meditate upon the brief reflection written in the devotional. All of these methods are wonderful ways to pray with the Word of God.

5 STEPS TO SUCCESSFUL HOME SCHOOLING

Lectio Divina

Quite possibly, one of the most enriching methods of praying with Scripture is called lectio divina, which is Latin for 'sacred reading'. This ancient method of prayer, preserved by the Benedictine monastic tradition, is believed to have been practiced routinely by all Christians at one time (Dysinger 1).

The most important fruit from the repeated practice of lectio divina is the ability to *listen* to God, which St. Benedict calls "hearing with the ears of our hearts" (Prologue, Rule of St. Benedict). Lectio divina consists of four simple steps - reading, meditation, prayer, and contemplation.

The first step involves reading a selected scripture verse or passage. Fr. Luke Dysinger, OSB, beautifully describes this step as "reverential listening; listening in a spirit of both silence and awe." He reminds us that we must not read the Bible in the same way that we read the newspaper, a magazine, or even our favorite book. Rather, we read with a listening ear (Dysinger 2). Reading the passage out loud may help you slow your pace and focus more clearly on the words (Pratt 182). In any case, keep reading the Scripture passage until a word, phrase, or idea catches your attention. At that point, pause and begin the second step of lectio divina, meditation.

To meditate, you ponder, ruminate, and 'chew' on the word or phrase that spoke directly to you. Lonni Collins Pratt, the author of *Benedict's Way*, says that you "spend time with it, roll it over, wrap yourself completely around it, and let it penetrate you to the core" (Pratt 182).

Next, during the intimate third step of lectio divina, you shift focus from yourself to God. Through prayer, you completely open your deepest self, offering Him your triumphs, failings, and deepest hurts.

STEP 1: PRAY

You "allow your real self to be touched and changed by the word of God" (Dysinger 2).

Finally, you move to the fourth step of lectio divina. In contemplation you simply rest in God's presence. Fr. Dysinger says, "No one who has ever been in love needs to be reminded that there are moments in loving relationships when words are unnecessary. It is the same in our relationship with God. Wordless, quiet rest in the presence of the One Who loves us has a name in the Christian tradition - contemplation. Once again, we practice silence" (Dysinger 3).

Some resources suggest re-reading the same Scripture passage a second time and even a third time to see if anything different catches our attention. This re-reading of the passage, often done in a group setting, can also be practiced alone in a single sitting, later in the day, or even over the course of three days. The goal in lectio divina is not to 'cover' a set amount of material over a certain number of days. Rather, it is to listen to the Word of God and allow it to penetrate your heart.

Learning to listen to God takes practice. Have you ever stopped to consider the amount of personal prayer time that is spent with *you* doing the talking? For any relationship to grow, including your relationship with Christ, communication must include both talking and listening. Lectio Divina is one way to develop this ability to listen to God.

Rote Prayer

Rote prayer is another method that offers many blessings to those who practice it regularly. Like Biblical prayer, rote prayer can enhance your spiritual growth. Whether you read the psalms, recite meaningful prayers written by the saints of old, or pray the rosary; all of these offer ample opportunity for you to unite your heart to God through meditation and contemplation. While reciting the familiar words of prayers such as the Lord's Prayer, the Hail Mary,

5 STEPS TO SUCCESSFUL HOME SCHOOLING

the Serenity Prayer, the Psalms, or the Prayer of St. Francis, you can carefully reflect upon them while listening to God as He speaks to you.

The Rosary

The rosary is one form of rote prayer that has played an important role in my life for the past few of years. According to "How to Pray the Holy Rosary," the Holy Rosary has been a treasured devotion in the Catholic Church for centuries. It is a deeply contemplative prayer that contains a summary of the Christian faith in language and prayers inspired by the Holy Scriptures. When praying the Rosary, you recall the most important events of the lives of Jesus and His Blessed Mother Mary (Lighthouse 5).

Although the rosary is often thought of as a strictly Catholic form of prayer, many Protestant Christians admit to gaining tremendous blessings by praying the rosary. In fact, in his book *Five for Sorrow, Ten for Joy*, the well known Methodist writer, J. Neville Ward, says:

> People unused to the rosary may hesitate over its most frequently repeated prayer – *Hail Mary, full of grace, the Lord is with thee. Blessed art thou among women, and blessed is the fruit of thy womb, Jesus. Holy Mary, Mother of God, pray for us sinners, now and at the hour of our death. Amen.*
>
> The first part of this prayer, from Luke 1:28 and 42, is a way of bringing to mind our belief that the Incarnation of the Son of God is the most wonderful thing that has ever happened in history, and therefore, restoring the mind to the joy which is at the foundation of the Christian life. It seems to me to be also particularly inspired in that our joy that God has revealed Himself to us is associated with his favouring and blessing another human being, so that a basis is laid in our regular prayer for our training in that happiness at God's blessing of other people which is such an important part of loving.

STEP 1: PRAY

The second part of the prayer is a reminder that Christ has abolished our loneliness, that we pray (even if alone at home or in an empty church) within the fabulous community of faith, live within it, owe more than we know to it, and particularly rely on the prayer of others, the whole communion of saints, of which the Blessed Virgin Mary is the representative figure.

The movement of the mind (while praying the rosary) between meditation and contemplation and petition and praise is a feature of this way of praying that gives it great flexibility and may well explain in part why it appeals to so many people so different in religious make-up (Coughlin 364-365).

To pray the rosary, you meditate, pray over, and contemplate the significant events in the life of Christ and His Holy Mother. These events are broken down into four sets of mysteries, each of which focuses on five different events. They are as follows:

The Joyful Mysteries
    1. The Annunciation (Lk 1:26-28, 38)
    2. The Visitation (Lk 1:39-41, 45)
    3. The Birth of our Lord (Lk 2:11)
    4. The Presentation in the Temple (Lk 2:27-30)
    5. The Finding in the Temple (Lk 2: 49-51)

The Luminous Mysteries
    1. The Baptism of Jesus (Mt 3:16-17)
    2. The Wedding Feast of Cana (Jn 2:3-5, 11)
    3. The Proclamation of the Kingdom (Mk 1:14-15)
    4. The Transfiguration (Lk 9:29-35)
    5. The Institution of the Eucharist (Mt 26:26-28)

The Sorrowful Mysteries
    1. The Agony in the Garden (Lk 22:42-43)
    2. The Scourging at the Pillar (Mk 15:15)

3. The Crowning with Thorns (Jn 19:1-2)
4. The Carrying of the Cross (Mt 27:31)
5. The Crucifixion (Lk 23:33-34,46)

The Glorious Mysteries
1. The Resurrection (Mt 28:6-7; 1Cor 15:21)
2. The Ascension (Acts 1:8, 9)
3. The Descent of the Holy Spirit (Acts 2:2, 4)
4. The Assumption of Mary (Judith 13:18, Eccl 24:9-10)
5. The Coronation of Our Blessed Mother (Rev 12:1, 5)

For more information on praying the rosary, please see the appendix, which lists all of the prayers recited during the rosary, and the order in which they are prayed. If you've never tried this form of prayer, I strongly encourage you to try it – even once. Pope John Paul II said, "Confidently take up the Rosary once again. Rediscover the Rosary in light of Scripture, in harmony with the Liturgy, and in the context of your daily lives" (Lighthouse).

Spontaneous Prayer

Spontaneous prayer is another form of prayer that can bring you and your home school many blessings. The word 'spontaneous' can refer to random points in time, meaning that whenever you think of it, you turn your heart toward God. Certainly, we are called to do this. How often, throughout the day, during difficult school lessons, after receiving phone calls of concern, or while enjoying God's creation during a walk on a beautiful day do I call upon God's help or offer up a quick prayer of petition or thanksgiving. Such prayers occur naturally and are not scheduled.

You should also schedule a time for spontaneous prayer. If you're thinking that scheduling defeats the purpose of this impromptu style of prayer, nothing could be further from the truth. By scheduling prayer time, no matter what method of prayer is used, you ensure that

STEP 1: PRAY

it does not get overlooked or skipped in the hectic busyness of your day.

What does scheduled spontaneous prayer look like? Well, it does not rely upon Scripture verses, devotionals, pre-written prayers or reflections. It comes directly from the heart. It is open conversation between you and God that reflects whatever is on your mind at that moment. Some people like to keep a journal of such prayers because the writing process itself is meditative.

Beginning spontaneous prayer can be difficult at times. Using the Lord's Prayer as a guide can be helpful. If you study this prayer you can see that it includes adoration, contrition, petition, and thanksgiving. Our prayers, too, should follow this pattern. According to Fr. Arnold Weber, OSB, in his book *Homilies for the Active Christian*, prayers of adoration acknowledge God as Almighty. Prayers of contrition acknowledge that we are all sinners and need mercy. Prayers of thanksgiving are those in which we give thanks to God for our many blessings. And prayers of supplication or petition are those in which we ask God for something. Adoration, contrition, petition, and thanksgiving should be the framework for all of our prayers.

Although spontaneous prayer comes from the heart, and is not pre-planned or pre-scripted, you will want to be certain that you remain focused in your prayers. According to Fr. Weber, the focus should be on God. We are to, "pray in fellowship with Him, so that His will can be done through us" (Weber 84). Fr. Weber illustrated the importance of staying focused with the following story:

> "Often our lives become cluttered – sometimes even with beautiful things – and we lose our focus on God. Once, a church purchased a beautiful statue of a saint. The environment committee found a place to put the statue. Then they purchased some beautiful flowers to place around the statue. The flowers were in full bloom and smelled lovely. A couple of candles were also added to the display. The

15

committee continued working to enhance the display. When the pastor walked by, they asked, "What do you think?" "It's great," he said, "but where's the statue?"

The environment committee had lost their focus. Their display became cluttered. The flowers were good and beautiful. The candles were lovely as well. But they added clutter, rather than focus. Our prayers need to remain focused on God as modeled in the Lord's Prayer" (Weber 85).

Adoration

Adoration of the Blessed Sacrament is another form of private prayer that you might consider doing regularly. If you live near a Catholic Church that has a Blessed Sacrament chapel that offers adoration, consider spending an hour each week in that chapel with our Lord.

As Bible believing Christians, Catholics believe in the true presence of Christ in the most Holy Communion. John's Gospel affirms this truth quite clearly.

"Amen, amen, I say to you, whoever believes in me has eternal life. I am the bread of life. Your ancestors ate the manna in the desert, but they died; this is the bread that comes down from heaven so that one may eat it and not die. I am the living bread that came down from heaven so that one may eat it and not die. I am the living bread that came down from heaven; whoever eats this bread will live forever; and the bread that I give is my flesh for the life of the world."

The Jews quarreled among themselves saying, "How can this man give us his flesh to eat?" Jesus said to them, "Amen, amen, I say to you, unless you eat the flesh of the Son of Man and drink his blood, you do not have life within you. Whoever eats my flesh and drinks my blood has eternal life, and I will raise him on the last day. For my flesh is true food, and my blood is true drink. Whoever eats my flesh and drinks my blood remains in me and I in him. Just as the living

Father sent me and I have life because of the Father, so also the one who feeds on me will have life because of me (Jn 6:47-58).

Jesus, Himself, tells us that He is present in the bread eaten at Mass. This very bread (the consecrated Host) is displayed in the monstrance of the Blessed Sacrament chapel, and those who wish can sit and pray in the life-giving presence of Christ Himself who is present in the humble form of bread. If you have never done so, find an adoration chapel at a Catholic Church near you and spend an hour with our Lord. It can be transforming!

PRAYER WITH OTHERS

Just as Christ demonstrated the need for private prayer, He also showed the importance of praying together. Whether at the temple, in the boat, in the garden, on the mountain, or at the table, Christ prayed with others. We, too, are called to pray in communion with others.

Fr. Patrick Peyton said, "The family that prays together, stays together" (Hahn 230). How true this is! Once my children and I are gathered in our home classroom, we start each day together with prayer. We also pray before meals, before bed, and often throughout our day together. My hope is to make prayer such a natural and common practice (just as my own parents did) that my children will bring it to their own homes some day.

All of the private forms of prayer just discussed – Biblical prayer, rote prayer, spontaneous prayer, and adoration – can be done individually or as a family. My husband and I have practiced them all with each of our children, selecting the method based upon the age of the child and the amount of time available. As the children have grown, certain prayer forms have become more effective than when they were younger. Introducing each method early in childhood (even in 'bite size pieces'), however, has made their practice easier and

5 STEPS TO SUCCESSFUL HOME SCHOOLING

more natural as the children have grown. For example, when praying the rosary as a family, we tried the following techniques to help when the children were young. First, we started with just a decade of the rosary. When we felt the children were old enough for more, we divided up parts by inviting the older children to take turns saying the "Our Father" and the "Hail Mary," the younger children would say the "Glory Be," while the youngest came in with every "Amen." As they've grown, we've invited some to read reflections before each mystery and others to lead different sections of prayer. It has been beautiful to see them grow in their understanding of the rosary, and watch their desire to participate in the prayers.

Let us now look at the highest form of communal prayer in our Christian tradition – the Mass, which the Catechism of the Catholic Church calls the "source and summit" of the Christian faith (CCC 1324).

The Mass

"Where do you want us to go and prepare for you to eat the Passover?" He sent two of his disciples and said to them, "Go into the city and a man will meet you, . . . Follow him. Then he will show you a large upper room furnished and ready. Make the preparations for us there (Mark 14:12b, 13, 15).

Then he took the bread, said the blessing, broke it, and gave it to them, saying, "This is my body which will be given for you; do this in memory of me" (Mark 14:22-26).

The Mass, with all of its richness, mystery, and grace comes to us from Jesus, Himself. Indeed, it was Christ who instituted the Eucharist, Christ who gave us the basic 'formula' for the Liturgy, and Christ who is still present with us at each and every Mass.

The Gospels tell us the story of the Last Supper. At this final meal before His Passion, not only did Our Lord institute the celebration

18

STEP 1: PRAY

of the Holy Sacrifice, He commanded His apostles – and us – to continue this sacrament in His memory.

The Church, in its deep love for Christ, has honored, respected, and lovingly obeyed this command for two thousand consecutive years. The Eucharist, which is Greek for 'thanksgiving', is our offering of thanks to God for sending His only Son to suffer and die for our sins, so that we might live (John 3:16).

Following the resurrection of our Lord, the story of Emmaus (Luke 24: 25-32) helps us to see where the general 'formula' for the Mass originated. On the road to Emmaus, Jesus approached two disciples who did not immediately recognize Him. He asked them what they were talking about and they told Him about the recent crucifixion of Jesus. He said to them in reply, "Oh, how foolish you are! How slow of heart to believe all that the prophets spoke!" Then, Jesus went on to recite Scripture for them, beginning with Moses. After reciting Scripture to His disciples, Jesus then interpreted it for them. Indeed, He gave them a homily. Even that was not enough, however, for the disciples to fully recognize Christ. After listening to Jesus for a while, they invited Him to eat with them, and *it was in the breaking of the bread that they recognized our Lord.*

Our Mass today follows this same basic formula given to us by Jesus at Emmaus. We begin with the Liturgy of the Word, which consists of multiple Scripture readings from the Old Testament, the Psalms, the New Testament letters, and the Gospels, that are then interpreted and explained by the Presider. (In the course of three years, faithful Catholics who attend Mass regularly will hear nearly the entire Bible.)

This is not enough, however, for it is in the breaking of the bread that Christ is truly made known and remains with us. Therefore, we follow this first part of the Mass (the Liturgy of the Word) with the Liturgy of the Eucharist, our sacrificial offering in union with Christ and our communion meal (Richards).

5 STEPS TO SUCCESSFUL HOME SCHOOLING

From the beginning, to be Christian was to go to Mass (Hahn 29). In the Early Church, the faithful went to the Temple to hear the Word of God. They would then gather in homes for the breaking of the bread. This continued until the destruction of the Temple in 70A.D. After the destruction, the early followers simply met in homes where they recited Scripture, listened to the letters written by the Apostles (which we now find in the New Testament), and broke the sacred bread together.

For us, as Catholic Christian home schooling parents, the value of keeping Mass a focal point of the week is immeasurable. Sadly, many parents today give other activities a higher priority than attending Mass. They skip the Sunday Celebration to attend hockey practice, soccer games, or basketball tournaments. Some even skip Mass simply to sleep in. How sad this is! There is no question that regular Mass attendance requires commitment and sometimes sacrifice. However, there is nothing more deserving of such effort.

Our family is blessed to live near a family who has offered us a beautiful example of what making an effort to get to Mass looks like. This family has seven children, all of whom are gifted athletes. As of this writing, the five older children are all involved in competitive travel sports twelve months of the year, playing at the highest level of competition for their age brackets. Yet, despite juggling five travel basketball, baseball, football, softball, and soccer schedules, this family attends Mass every single week of the year! Such dedication to their faith takes effort, creativity, and commitment. Sometimes the whole family attends Mass in the city that is hosting the baseball tournament, even if they have to get there between tournament games. Other weeks, they may divide up as a family, some going to the early Mass, and others later. What an example they are to their teammates, neighbors, and other parishioners! Imagine if everyone would make even half the effort of this family. Our churches would be filled every week!

STEP 1: PRAY

We have tried very hard to instill a strong commitment to the faith in our children. Although it takes commitment and sacrifice, we do not want church to feel like drudgery or punishment. We've always tried to make going to Mass something to look forward to – even when the children were too young to appreciate its true value. For example, when we first started home schooling, my plan was to attend one daily Mass every week, as the older kids did when they went to Catholic school. Some of our children were quite young, however, and sitting though two Masses each week was difficult. So, after daily Mass, we began stopping by a store near the church where we would each choose and eat a freshly baked donut. Occasionally, other church going friends would join us. After seven years, we are still enjoying these donuts and we have come to know many of the workers at the store quite well!

A year or so after we began this donut tradition, another home schooling mother asked the priest at our small church if some of us could organize a weekly home school Mass, and he agreed. On Friday mornings, our kids participate in Mass by reading the daily Scriptures and the responsorial Psalm. They also act as altar servers. Friday morning Mass attendance has skyrocketed as more and more Catholic home schooling families have joined us. My kids look forward to Friday morning Mass for many reasons, especially the wonderful fellowship. They enjoy worshiping with their friends during Mass and socializing with them after.

Whether or not you home educate your children, I strongly encourage you to make Mass attendance a priority. Your family will be greatly blessed as a result.

PRAY FIRST

As mentioned at the start of this chapter, before beginning His public ministry, Jesus went into the desert to pray. We, too, need to begin

21

5 STEPS TO SUCCESSFUL HOME SCHOOLING

with prayer each and every day. Before rushing into your school agenda - math lessons, field trips, or research projects, consider seeking God's wisdom and guidance. This may require setting your alarm clock fifteen minutes earlier than usual, but it will be well worth it!

First and foremost, praying before you undertake any task puts God in control. Before deciding to home school, pray. Before choosing curriculum materials, pray. At the beginning of each day, pray. Listen to God's wisdom and receive the grace necessary to accomplish the enormous task of educating your children.

A few years ago, while reading Holly Pierlot's book, *A Mother's Rule of Life,* I made a personal commitment to start each day in prayer. Pierlot's book described Mother Teresa's daily schedule which began at 4:30am! After rising and washing up, Mother Teresa and the other Missionaries of Charity spent the next 1½ hours in Mass and additional prayer time before beginning their humanitarian service work (Pierlot 15). This greatly inspired me to want to do more than I was doing at the time (which was nothing). I desired to schedule prayer time at the start of each day. I was realistic, however, in knowing myself. I am not an early riser. Setting the alarm for 4:30am to spend 1½ hours in prayer is something I could probably accomplish once, but not something I could do every day. So, I was relieved and further motivated when I saw that Pierlot's day began at 6:45am and allowed about twenty minutes of personal prayer time (Pierlot 20). That seemed like something I could manage.

My morning routine has evolved into morning Mass attendance or praying the rosary while walking the dog before starting our school day. This daily commitment has taken some discipline, but is well worth the effort and has enriched my prayer life greatly. During the summer when the weather is warm and we are not schooling, I really enjoy this morning prayer walk. In the winter, however, when we have early morning commitments and it is cold outside, I am often tempted to skip the whole routine. It requires a much greater level

STEP 1: PRAY

of discipline and commitment. (Incidentally, when the temperature drops lower than five degrees below zero, I do skip the walk, but not the prayer.)

Once you've done your private prayer, don't forget to pray with your children, after they're up, dressed, fed, and the breakfast dishes are put away. Before diving into the daily grammar lesson, read from the Bible, pray spontaneously, or recite some rote prayers together. One method of prayer I strongly encourage is to read the Sunday Scripture readings aloud with your children the week prior to hearing them at Mass. Allow the children to take turns reading them. Discuss the stories and their meanings with them throughout the week. Being familiar with the readings they will hear at the Sunday celebration will go a long way in your child's recognition of the Word and their understanding of Mass.

Whichever method you choose, even if you choose a different method of prayer each day, stay consistent in that you pray before beginning the work day. Model this behavior by praying alone, and then teach your children to pray by praying with them. What an excellent way to start the day!

PRAY OFTEN

"Will not God then secure the rights of his chosen ones who call out to him day and night?" (Luke 18:7a)

As the title of this book suggests, there are five steps to successful home schooling. Prayer is the first step. However, if you pray one fervent prayer on the first day of school and then never pray again, you will not see the same benefits as with daily consistency.

Decide *now* what your regular commitment to prayer will look like and then do it. Mother Teresa spent more than three hours each day

5 STEPS TO SUCCESSFUL HOME SCHOOLING

in scheduled prayer. Benedictine monks come together at regular intervals throughout each day - morning, noon, evening, and night. This level of commitment to prayer may not be realistic for you (and I have not achieved this yet either), so begin with a schedule that is doable for you and stick with it.

If you are just beginning your prayer journey, consider aiming for fifteen minutes at the start of each day, every day for one year. *Then, let God grow your prayer life.* Your prayer life will be, and should be, unique. Be careful not to compare yourself to others. Your friend might pray five hours a day while wearing sack cloth. That might be what God is calling her to do, but He may not be calling you to do the same. Listen to God's voice. He will lead you if you let Him.

Home educating offers many blessings and challenges. Through home schooling, we have the privilege of helping our children learn while we learn along with them. You will share their triumphs as they master reading, long division, and spelling new words. You'll also share in their frustration when they struggle with sentence diagramming, algebra, and general science. Some days you'll have more energy and be a better teacher than you will on other days. Certain lessons or subjects will come easier, while some will be difficult. Some of your children will learn faster than others. They'll go through different stages of child development, some of which will warm your heart and others which will turn your hair gray. Throughout it all, God is by your side. He will make this journey with you, guiding, refining, and helping you, if you let Him. So before undertaking this noble task of home schooling, be sure to pray.

STEP 1: PRAY!

1. Pray alone, then pray with others. Both are important!

2. Pray first. Start each day in prayer.

3. Pray often. Consider times throughout the day when you can add prayer. Allow God to lead.

STEP 2:
ESTABLISH YOUR MISSION

"I continue my pursuit toward the goal, the prize of God's upward calling, in Christ Jesus. Let us, then, who are 'perfectly mature' adopt this attitude." (Philippians 3:14-15)

So, why *are* you home schooling or considering home schooling? If you're just starting out, what do you hope to gain by home educating your children? If you have already been educating your children at home, have you succeeded? How do you know? For most of us who home school, the general goal is to be successful. If you aren't striving for success, then you probably shouldn't be educating your children at home. But what exactly is success? And, how do you know if you've achieved it?

Perhaps considering what is meant by 'education' will help to focus your thoughts on your definition of 'success'. Webster's New World Dictionary (Third College Edition) describes the word 'educate' as follows: *To train or develop the knowledge, skill, mind, or character of, esp. by formal schooling or study; teach; instruct.*

Therefore, if you train your children in character and mind, have you succeeded in your role as home educator? Can you measure this level of success? If your eight year old child learns to read, knows how to

add and subtract, watches the life cycle of a leaf on a tree, and can
retell some Bible stories with zeal, is this success? What if that same
child scores poorly on the required standardized tests? If your teen
is respectful, hardworking, and honest; does this indicate success?
What if your high school student receives high scores on their SAT
test, but has never volunteered for anything, is this success?

These are critical questions to ask before you begin to home school
your children. Many people are eager to jump into curriculum
options, look for co-ops, and dive into field trips. All of these
activities are important. However, before any of this can be done, I
encourage you to articulate your overall mission for home schooling.
Carole Joy Seid, a popular speaker within the world of home
education, offers a seminar titled, "Beginning With the End in
Mind." Her talk sums up the reasons for establishing a mission
statement before starting to home school your children. Articulating
your reasons for home schooling and what your overall goals are is
important before beginning to educate your children.

Indeed, you need to know the direction in which you hope to head
before setting off on this journey. If you don't have any idea where
you want to go, you may end up somewhere that you don't want to
be. A home school mission statement is like the address (the final
destination) you plug into the GPS system in your car. It will help
you start off in the right direction, and even if you come across
roadblocks and need to detour along the way, you can still arrive at
your desired destination.

Yes, you need to know what your overall plan and long range
objectives are for Sally or Tommy before deciding which grammar
program she should use in second grade or which extracurricular
activities he should participate in as a teenager. That way, you can
select the grammar program and extracurricular activities that will
best help them to achieve their objectives. In her essay, "The Lost
Tools of Learning," Dorothy Sayers questions, "What use is it to pile
task on task and prolong the days of labor, if at the close the chief

STEP 2: ESTABLISH YOUR MISSION

objective is left unattained?" Not until you establish your long range goals can you properly organize your home school curriculum and calendar. With firm priorities in mind, you'll be intentional about scheduling the most beneficial activities first before tasks of lesser importance fill up the time your family has available.

Many home school people agree that it is a good idea to have a mission statement, yet they don't take time to actually write one out. Even many families who have home educated their children for years will admit that they've never put on paper what has been in their minds. This was true for me at first. It wasn't until after two years of home schooling, that I began to articulate some well thought out academic, social, physical, emotional, and spiritual goals for each of my children. After this exercise, I felt I had done a good job at looking at the development of each child as an individual and assessed growth areas for each of them. What I neglected to do, however, was look at the family as a whole. I did not have a mission statement that reflected the values, goals, and principles of our family as a unit. There is a difference.

This became evident to me as I looked into ways for my children to attain the goals I had outlined for them. Scheduling activities, purchasing curriculum materials, and volunteering for events required time and money from the family resources. My husband and I realized that we needed to discuss what our family goals were related to our finances and our time. We needed to ask questions such as: How many evenings do we want to have family dinners? How much money is available for school related materials? How much money is available for sports and other activities? What family activities are important to us? What family obligations do we have? How does each of the children's activities impact the family as a whole?

Today, our mission statement provides focus and direction for everything that goes on in our home. It also provides a basis for planning and decision-making, including those related to home

5 STEPS TO SUCCESSFUL HOME SCHOOLING

schooling (and the individual goals for our children).

Without question, a mission statement is an essential part of your home education program. So, what should your mission statement be? Well, I wish I knew. Imagine the books I could sell if I knew the magic mission statement that worked for every family! Unfortunately, that's not how it works. Because the individual make-up, personality, and aspirations of every family are unique, each family needs its own mission statement. The mission statements of any two families may be similar to one another, but rarely will they be identical. There are some basic steps, however, that you can follow to create your family's personal mission statement.

ASK THE RIGHT QUESTIONS

First and foremost, when preparing a family mission statement, be sure to ask the right questions. This story, delivered in a homily by Fr. Arnold Weber, OSB, and documented in his book, *Homilies for the Active Christian,* illustrates why:

> Friends, one of the most crucial problems today is finding the meaning in life! So many people are disappointed because they say life has no meaning. Well, what is the meaning of life? Can I decide that for you? Most would say not. So how, then, do you find the right answer?
>
> I think we have to start by asking the right questions. Some get the right answers to the wrong questions, and then wonder why they're missing out on a meaningful life. For example, a young man goes to college and tries to decide in what area to focus his studies. So he asks himself, "What career will give me the most money?" He might get the right answer to that question and make millions, but be disappointed in the end.

STEP 2: ESTABLISH YOUR MISSION

A lot of unhappy people would eagerly trade their success for peace and happiness. What goes wrong? They find the right answer to the wrong question (Weber 31-32).

Indeed, before you write your mission statement, you need to think about and ask some very important questions. First, what exactly is a mission statement? Wikipedia, the free on-line encyclopedia defines *mission statement* as, "a formal, short, written statement of the purpose of a company or organization. The mission statement should guide the actions of the organization, spell out its overall goal, provide a sense of direction, and guide decision making. It provides the 'framework or context within which the company's strategies are formulated.'" Janet M. Radtke states that, "a good mission statement should accurately explain why your organization exists and what it hopes to achieve in the future. It articulates the organization's essential nature, its values, and its work" (Radtke 1).

Other questions related to home schooling that you may wish to think about include:
1. Why are we home schooling?
2. What is our family's definition of success as it relates to home schooling?
3. What academic skills do we want our children to acquire before they graduate? What knowledge should they have?
4. How important is our faith to us? What role do we want it to play in the education of our children?
5. How can we instill a love for learning in our children?
6. What practical skills do we want our children to learn?
7. What relationship skills do we hope they will acquire?
8. What character traits do we want our children to develop?
9. Against what criteria do we make our decisions regarding curriculum, clubs, and activities?

These questions will give you a good starting point. Ponder them. Take them to the Lord and ask the Holy Spirit to give you and your family wisdom and discernment. Discuss them with your spouse and, depending on their ages, with your children. Dr. Stephen Covey, author of *Seven Habits of Highly Effective Families* recommends including the children in the process of writing the mission statement. He says, "The key is not to ignore the children's input and just present the mission statement to them. They must feel they helped to produce it" (Covey 2).

A friend of mine with twin high school age daughters mentioned that they are in the process of writing a mission statement. She said, "We have had one family meeting and some interesting discussion. We are seeing this as an interesting process and I think it will take a couple more get-togethers before we have a final product. I think we will find as much, if not more, value in the process as in the final product."

WRITE YOUR OWN MISSION STATEMENT

In addition to asking the right questions within your family, ask trusted friends if they would be willing to share their home school mission statements (if they have them) with you. It is also a good idea to look through home school books and periodicals that you respect for examples of mission statements. Reading other mission statements can give you ideas that will help you in writing your own.

Below are some examples of mission statements that can serve as a starting point for you as you write your own. Read through them, share them with your spouse and children, and borrow whatever is appropriate for your own mission statement.

    1. I want eternal salvation for my children. I want to teach the appropriate disciplines at the right ages for each child to reach maximum benefits. I want my children to be able to go to an academically excellent Catholic college and do well there. I want to instill an attitude about learning

STEP 2: ESTABLISH YOUR MISSION

that would lead to real interest in all parts and aspects of God's creation. Finally, the moral virtues must become habits in the children and in me. (Paraphrased from Laura Berquist's book *Designing Your Own Catholic Curriculum*)

2. We want our home school to teach responsibility, virtue, faith, and academic knowledge while exuding joy. We want our home school to offer challenge in both academic and character development. We want to provide an environment of encouragement. We want our children to become life long learners who develop into adults of integrity, intelligence, and faith. We want our children to put faith and family first, while participating in the greater community as responsible citizens.

3. Our home school will help our children grow into adults of faith. Through a Christian world view, we will instruct our children in the academic disciplines necessary to develop into critical thinkers. Our children will master communication skills so as to communicate effectively in both the written and the spoken word. Our children will learn what is necessary to be healthy in the areas of faith, mind, body, and finances, and how to maintain health in those areas as adults.

4. Our home school mission is to provide the children a loving environment to learn, to explore, to grow, to question, and to take ownership of their education. Each child will be given the opportunity to be taught in the manner that is best for their unique learning style. They will also be encouraged to explore areas of interest including academics, sports, theater, art, music, faith, literature, home economics, and the like. We will ensure that the children are taught the true teachings of the Catholic Church. The ultimate goal is that each child

33

5 STEPS TO SUCCESSFUL HOME SCHOOLING

will be well rooted with the character and values of the Catholic faith and of their parents, allowing them to confidently enter society, at the appropriate age for each, and succeed.

After you've considered the important questions, studied some examples of mission statements, and done a lot of praying, it is time to put pen to paper and write out your own mission statement. Make it as short as possible – two pages is too long. Home school parents tend to want to do it all – and have our children know all and excel at all. Unfortunately, that is not possible. Narrow your focus to those things that are of highest priority to your family.

Once your mission statement is written, go back to the definitions of 'mission statement' to ensure that yours includes all of the main elements. Does your mission statement accurately state your over all long range goals as home educators? Does it provide direction for your task as a home schooling parent? Does it mention your values? Is it brief? Is it agreed upon by the members of your family? If so, then it's time to put together your home education plan!

CREATE A HOME SCHOOL PLAN

After you've established your long range goals, the next question to ask is, "How do we achieve these goals?" If you have ever taken a marketing class, you will probably realize that what you need to do next is to identify the strategies that will lead to achievement of the objectives. A typical marketing outline looks like this:

    I. Objective #1
        a. Strategy
            i. Tactic
            ii. Tactic
        b. Strategy
            i. Tactic

STEP 2: ESTABLISH YOUR MISSION

              ii. Tactic
        c. Strategy
              i. Tactic
              ii. Tactic

II. Objective #2
        a. Strategy
              i. Tactic
              ii. Tactic
        b. Strategy
              i. Tactic
              ii. Tactic
        c. Strategy
              i. Tactic
              ii. Tactic
III. Objective #3
        a. Strategy
              i. Tactic
              ii. Tactic
        b. Strategy
              i. Tactic
              ii. Tactic
        c. Strategy
              i. Tactic
              ii. Tactic

Let's take a look at how this marketing plan format can be used for putting together an effective home school program that, over the years, will help you achieve the long term objectives you have for your children. Once you have this program in place, it can be reviewed and adapted periodically or on a per child basis to meet his or her specific needs.

We'll use the first mission statement example as our guide, and prepare an outline based upon the goals that it espouses.

5 STEPS TO SUCCESSFUL HOME SCHOOLING

Objective #1 = I want eternal salvation for my children.

> *Strategy: Teach the faith to our children*
>> Tactic: Find a solid religion curriculum program and include it as one of the academic subjects taught throughout the week.
>>
>> Tactic: Look into faith formation programs at our church and consider enrolling our children in these programs.
>>
>> Tactic: Prepare them for the sacraments.

> *Strategy: Live the faith*
>> Tactic: Pray as a family.
>>> a. Model prayer.
>>> b. Teach prayers to the children.
>>
>> Tactic: Read the Bible.
>>> a. Introduce Bible stories.
>>> b. Practice Bible verse memorization.
>>> c. Consider Bible studies for older children.
>>
>> Tactic: Make Mass a priority.
>>> a. Attend Sunday Mass.
>>> b. Consider attending daily Mass.
>>
>> Tactic: Look into faith centered social groups and consider participating.
>>> a. Little Flowers.
>>> b. Blue Knights.
>>> c. Youth groups offered through our church or diocese.
>>> d. Consider forming a Catholic based social group that meets the needs of our child/children.

> *Strategy: Use curriculum materials in all subjects that are written with a Catholic world view.*
>> Tactic: Investigate different Catholic home school programs and materials. (See Appendix B)

36

STEP 2: ESTABLISH YOUR MISSION

     a. Laura Berquist's book *Designing Your
     Own Classical Curriculum.*
     b. Mother of Divine Grace Home School
     Program.
     c. Seton Home School.
     d. Kolbe Academy.
     e. Our Lady of Victory School.
     f. The Institute for Excellence in Writing.
     g. Others (see Appendix B).

Obviously, attaining eternal salvation is not something that will be achieved in one year of home schooling. It is a life long process. If this is a goal you have for your children, the steps listed above will help point them in the right direction and give them a strong foundation of faith on which to build. The strategies and tactics you choose to employ for your shy first grader, however, may be different from the strategies and tactics that you use for your out-going middle school age child. Furthermore, not every tactic needs to be tackled every year for each child. Later in this chapter we will take a look at annual goals that you may have for each child and how to apply the mission statement and overall plan to those personalized, individual goals.

Objective #2 = I want to teach the appropriate disciplines at the right ages for each child to reach maximum benefits.

> *Strategy: Identify which disciplines are 'appropriate' and necessary for elementary, middle school, and high school students.*
>
>   <u>Tactic:</u> Check with state board of education to learn what my state's requirements are. (See Step 5: Find Support for listing of local home school agencies).
>   <u>Tactic:</u> Read recommended home school books that outline curriculum guidelines (See next chapter for book recommendations).
>   <u>Tactic:</u> Review Catholic home school programs to

5 STEPS TO SUCCESSFUL HOME SCHOOLING

determine which subjects are recommended at the different age levels. (See Appendix B).

Tactic: Determine in which areas of study I have a strong interest.

Tactic: Determine those areas of study that are of strong interest to my child.

Strategy: Learn how to recognize when my child is most ready for a certain level of study.

Tactic: Read recommended books on child development, temperament, and learning styles (See next chapter).

Tactic: Attend home school conferences and other home education workshops in my area. Often, this is a topic of one or more of the workshops. (See Step 5: Find Support for listing of local agencies)

Tactic: Talk with other home schooling parents in my area.

Objective #3 = I want my children to go to an academically excellent Catholic college and do well there.

Strategy: Beginning in middle school, research colleges and find out what their admission requirements are (especially for home educated students).

Tactic: Go on-line to college websites.

Tactic: Meet with college counselors at local high school.

Tactic: Consider visiting a selected college and meet with someone from their admissions department.

Strategy: Prepare a plan of action for all four years of high school that meets the admission requirements.

Tactic: Determine what course work is required.

a. Establish schedule for completing required classes.

38

STEP 2: ESTABLISH YOUR MISSION

        b. Determine the best way for each class to be taught (i.e. by the parent, by a tutor, on-line, or through an outside class).

Tactic: Plan to take required standardized tests.
        a. PLAN, PSAT, SAT, ACT
        b. AP tests
        c. CLEP tests

Tactic: Review extracurricular activities and consider addressing areas that are important according to college admission requirements and the interests of my child.
        a. Volunteer work
        b. Jobs
        c. Sports involvement
        d. Leadership roles
        e. Drama, speech, debate
        f. Music
        g. Other

Strategy: Talk with other home school parents whose children have been accepted into the desired colleges.

Tactic: Attend Catholic home school conferences.

Tactic: Look for and attend workshops on home educating through high school. (See Step 4: Find Support)

Tactic: Talk with other home school parents or tutors in my area.

Objective #4 = I want to instill an attitude about learning that would lead to real interest in all parts and aspects of God's creation.

Strategy: Carefully examine my own attitude about teaching and learning and look for ways to maintain my energy and enthusiasm.

Tactic: Be certain I am modeling the behavior I hope my children to gain.

5 STEPS TO SUCCESSFUL HOME SCHOOLING

Tactic: Schedule times throughout the day for rest and prayer to help maintain my energy level.
Tactic: Enlist the help of my children with household chores.

Strategy: Look for fun and creative ways to learn (that take us out of the textbook).
Tactic: Field trips
Tactic: Great literature (read alouds, audio books, drama performances of literature that tie in with other areas of our studies).
Tactic: Family vacations that tie in with what we are learning in some area of our studies (i.e. history, science, geography, or literature).
Tactic: Education games
Tactic: Science experiments
Tactic: The arts
Tactic: Book clubs

Strategy: Be a continual learner myself.
Tactic: Read every day.
Tactic: Attend conferences, classes, and workshops (in the area of home education and other areas of interest to me).

Objective #5 = The moral virtues must become habits in the children and in me.

Strategy: Learn what the moral virtues are.
Tactic: Consider doing this together as a family.

Strategy: Look for ways to practice these virtues inside the home together as a family and as individuals.
Tactic: Consider praying more as a family.
Tactic: Consider reading the Bible more often as a family.

40

STEP 2: ESTABLISH YOUR MISSION

Tactic: Look on-line or at Catholic book stores for creative games, activities, and charts that help us learn and practice virtue.

Tactic: Review household responsibilities of everyone in the family and determine if the tasks/chores are being completed in a way that demonstrates virtue.

Strategy: Look for ways to practice virtue outside the home as a family and as individuals.

Tactic: Consider monthly confession.

Tactic: Consider more frequent Mass attendance.

Tactic: Look for volunteer opportunities within our church, neighborhood, and community.

Tactic: Look for ways within my neighborhood, church community, and home school community that I can humbly practice these virtues on a regular basis through my actions and words.

This is an example of what a home school plan to achieve the goals outlined in the first mission statement might look like. Your mission statement may be similar (but not identical) to this example, therefore your plan may have some similarities to this one, but will also have strategies and tactics unique to your family and goals.

If you carefully read through the plan, you will probably notice that there is a lot of work to be done if you want to accomplish your goals. That's the reality. Home educating children is a lot of work, and there's no way around that. But remember, it all doesn't (and shouldn't) have to be completed in one day.

If you haven't already done so, create a home school education plan now! If necessary, take a week off from schooling, or schedule time over the next four weekends to work on this project. Another good time to start would be before or after a home school conference. Truthfully, any time is good to begin thinking of your long term

41

5 STEPS TO SUCCESSFUL HOME SCHOOLING

goals and how you will successfully achieve them. It may seem tedious to write out a plan. The value of having a plan in place, however, is more than worth the effort it takes to complete it. Keep it in a notebook, three ring binder, or file folder where it will be handy when you learn about new classes, curriculum materials, or activities. Then, you'll be able to efficiently check these new ideas against your plan ("Will it help us achieve our goals?"), sign up for those that are appropriate, and order materials or supplies as necessary.

REVIEW YOUR PLAN

Once your mission statement is written, make sure to review it and update it (if necessary) every few years. However, your home education plan to achieve the goals of the mission statement must be reviewed often and updated continually.

Whether you are new to home schooling or have taught your children at home for many years, review your home education plan on a regular basis. Annual, mid-year (even mid-month or mid-week) adjustments may all be part of your home schooling. It is not uncommon for one math curriculum to work beautifully for one of your children, and not at all for another with a different learning style. Similarly, a daily schedule that works when your children are in elementary school may not work as well when some of them reach middle school or high school. Activities, too, will need to be adjusted based upon the requirements of your family during any given season. One of the beauties of home schooling is that you can adjust and tailor programs to fit the specific needs of your children and family. If something isn't working properly, you can fix it!

Ideally, review your plan quarterly; at a minimum every semester. When reviewing your home education plan, ask yourself:
1. Is the plan, as we've put it into practice, working for our family?

STEP 2: ESTABLISH YOUR MISSION

2. Are we trying to do too much? Should we discontinue any activity for anyone in the family?
3. Could we be doing more in any area of the plan?
4. Is there any area of the plan that we have not yet addressed? If so, when will we address it?
5. Do the activities in which we participate help us achieve the goals of our mission?
6. Are we involved in activities that prevent us from following our plan? If so, should these activities be discontinued?
7. How am I doing with my responsibilities? (Prayer, rest, reading, planning, organizing, educating, etc.)
8. What individual goals do I have for each of my children and how can this plan help me meet those goals?

As mentioned earlier, your home education plan can help your family meet the objectives mentioned in the mission statement. It identifies specific strategies and tactics to help the children achieve the overall goals you've set; which in our example were to gain eternal salvation, learn the faith, learn academics, get into a Catholic college, and instill a love for learning while practicing virtue. Detours may arise along the way, and some changes may need to be made. However, with your mission statement and home school plan close at hand, you will know your destination and can focus on achieving those overall goals.

In addition to long range goals for your home school, individual goals for each child are necessary and important. I spend a great deal of time in thought and prayer during the summer months to discern the needs and goals for each of my children for the upcoming year. Then, I plan certain strategies and tactics for each child based upon the goals I have established for them. For example, when my son was in sixth grade, some of the goals I had for him included:

Grow in faith
Maintain strong friendships
Continue with sports to level of enjoyment
Increase amount of reading

43

5 STEPS TO SUCCESSFUL HOME SCHOOLING

Become more self guided in more subject areas
Maintain high level of performance in all academic areas
Complete one volunteer activity each semester

The goals for my first grader were very different. They included:
Learn to read
Learn phonograms
Learn first grade prayers
Understand addition and subtraction
Learn to write all letters and simple sentences
Begin learning basic grammar
Help her to make one new friend
Introduce her to science and history

If the example mission statement and home education plan listed earlier were my own, obviously I wouldn't need to contact colleges, review college preparation tests, and look into job opportunities for my first grader. However, I could certainly use Catholic based reading programs to teach her to read. Making Mass a priority, attending home school conferences, and carefully selecting grammar, math and reading programs appropriate to her age and ability would definitely be tactics to employ. As for my sixth grader, his needs had more to do with growing in maturity. We continued with our carefully selected academic curriculum materials, but we also looked at ways for him to develop leadership skills, virtue, and enjoyment through learning.

Each year it is important to carefully ponder the needs and growth areas of each of your children, and review your plan carefully to select strategies and tactics to help them achieve these objectives. Not every tactic will be used for each child each year. Over the course of their years of schooling, however, you will feel confident having a road map in place to help guide your decisions along the way.

As we mentioned earlier, the home schooling movement has grown

44

STEP 2: ESTABLISH YOUR MISSION

rapidly within the past fifteen to twenty years. There is a plethora of materials, activities, classes, co-ops, books, curricula, and ideas to choose from. My first trip to a home school conference a few months before we began home educating our children was completely overwhelming. It was mind boggling to see more math, writing, grammar, and reading programs than I could count. There were bands to join, debate teams to sign up for, book clubs, sport teams, language clubs, literature programs, science curricula, science classes, science fairs, and science clubs. And this was just in the vendor area! There were also workshops and speakers discussing everything you could imagine: teaching your child to read, teaching algebra, growing spiritually, home schooling on a budget, healthy eating, maintaining a strong marriage, incorporating literature into your home school curriculum, the value of including art, the different learning styles of children, how to educate children with special needs, how to educate boys, and why classical music is of value! I wandered aimlessly through the vendor aisle before asking a few friends which workshops they recommended. Since I was feeling so lost and overwhelmed, I decided it was best not to make any purchases at that conference. I recognized, even then, the need for some sort of a plan before making decisions. I needed a mission, direction, and focus. And so do you.

Establishing a mission and creating a home education plan for achieving your goals will give you direction and purpose. Be intentional about completing this step. It will definitely help you achieve success on your home schooling journey. Just remember the saying, "When we fail to plan, we are planning to fail."

STEP 2:
ESTABLISH YOUR MISSION

1. Ask the right questions!

2. Write a mission statement that defines your goals for home education.

3. Create a home education plan. Determine strategies and tactics to achieve your goals.

4. Review your plan regularly. Adjust according to specific needs of each child.

STEP 3:
READ QUALITY LITERATURE

"Finally, brothers, whatever is true, whatever is honorable, whatever is just, whatever is pure, whatever is lovely, whatever is gracious, if there is any excellence and if there is anything worthy of praise, think about these things." (Philippians 4:8-9)

When my oldest was in kindergarten, he attended a lovely Catholic school near our home which hosted a book fair mid-way through the year. Like all enthusiastic mothers, I attended the fair eager to purchase some great books for my son. Once there, however, I just stared at all of the resources available, suddenly aware that I had no idea which books he would like or what I should be reading to him.

Growing up, I never read much. I remember hearing about (but never reading) *Heidi* or *Black Beauty* or *Tom Sawyer*. I never read *The Last of the Mohicans, Little Women, Where the Red Fern Grows,* or *Little Lord Fauntleroy*. I didn't know about C.S. Lewis, Maud Hart Lovelace, or J.R.R. Tolkien. Unbelievably, I never even read a single *Little House on the Prairie* book! So at that book fair, I really didn't know where to begin.

It was humbling to realize, while scanning the myriad of choices, that I didn't know which books were age appropriate for my son or even recommended. Without a doubt, this was an area in which my knowledge was inadequate. Over the next few years, however, I did little to learn about good books for children, other than ask a handful of friends here and there which books their children read as kindergarteners, first graders or second graders.

My introduction to the wonderful world of great literature began when we started home schooling our children. Reading together and discussing good literature has been a regular part of our school day from the start, and next to spending so much quality time together, it has been one of the greatest blessings to come from our home schooling adventure.

Anyone who attends a home schooling conference or spends any time at all time with home schooling families will quickly learn that most are passionate about great literature. Indeed, curriculum materials incorporate literature into history, science, language arts, faith formation, and even math programs! Home school parents have formed book clubs for their children and for themselves. Drama clubs perform productions based upon great literature. Speech classes pull interpretive pieces from excellent books. Grammar books teach comma usage, contraction rules, and the nuts and bolts of sentence diagramming based upon works of poetry and prose created by the greatest writers of all time.

In home educating our children, I've discovered a wealth of books that I never knew existed. Navigating through the world of excellent literary opportunity is easy, exciting, and enriching. The rest of this chapter provides some ideas to help you and your family step onto the path filled with great reading adventure!

Believe in the Value of Reading

Once you start reading together (if you haven't already), the value of this practice will become as obvious to you as why you exercise or follow a healthy diet. Following are just a few of the exceptional benefits that come from reading with your children and teaching them to read on their own:

Reading teaches the children about the world around them

Through books, children can learn about far off lands, people of different times, scientific discoveries, nature, the history of our nation and world, and even about family life. When children absorb information from exciting books, rather than from dull text books filled with facts to memorize, what they learn sticks with them. Indeed, they become so engaged in the stories and excited to find out what happens next, that they don't even realize they are learning! Charlotte Mason, a pioneer in the world of education, once stated,
> "The most common and monstrous defect in the education of the day is that children fail to acquire the habit of reading. Knowledge is conveyed to them by lessons and talk, but the studious habit of using books as a means of interest and delight is not acquired. This habit should begin early. . . . Once the habit of reading his lesson-books* with delight is set up in a child, his education is not completed, it is ensured" (Macaulay p.28, 32).
> * Note: The 'lesson-books' referred to are literature books, not text books!

Great literature can teach children more effectively than the most comprehensive of classroom textbooks. And what a teacher student ratio we achieve through reading - one teacher (the book) to one student! When children read great books, they learn about every aspect of the world around them through story-telling, an ancient, powerful form of instruction, and they retain the information because they remember it in the context of the story.

Historical fiction, biographies, and literature written during specific time periods are excellent ways to learn about history. Books about scientists or novels in which nature plays a role can teach more about the scientific world than most classroom textbooks because they engage the child's imagination and senses.

Through books, children also learn about social skills and behavior. They experience situations and circumstances that they have not yet experienced in their lives and see the consequences that result from the choices and actions of the various characters. As stated by children's author Barbara Freedman-DeVito, "Through stories and novels, children can vicariously try out new experiences and test new ideas, with no negative consequences in their real lives. Books also give kids the opportunity to flex their critical thinking skills in such areas as problem solving, the concepts of cause and effect, conflict resolution, and acceptance of responsibility for one's actions." (DeVito)

Reading teaches children about language

The more you read, the broader your vocabulary becomes; if you read a variety of well written books, magazines, newspapers, and other publications. (A plethora of dumbed-down reading material currently fills the shelves of children's and teen reading aisles, however, and a steady diet of this will not yield the same benefits as reading quality literature.) Regular reading of good books and periodicals will not only improve vocabulary, it will also increase knowledge of proper sentence structure and spelling. Children see and become familiar with the proper spelling of both common and unusual words. They learn about word meaning (often through sentence context), and see correct sentence structure. They see proper punctuation and capitalization.

STEP 3: READ QUALITY LITERATURE

Reading out loud to children (even teenage children) or having them listen to good audio books offers additional benefits. It allows them the opportunity to hear properly written English. In addition, through reading aloud, they learn to listen to the cadence and harmony of beautifully written language. Alliteration, rhyme, and poetic patterns come to life when recited. Most home education experts recommend reading aloud to your children (even teens) every day.

Reading offers entertainment

Another benefit to reading is that it can provide your children with hours of wonderful, enriching entertainment. How quickly many will turn on the television, iPod, electronic gaming device, and computer when looking for fun, unless they've discovered the pleasure offered by good books, board games, or the great outdoors.

A year after we began home schooling, we took a family road trip from Minnesota to the Grand Canyon. We clocked more than 90 hours of drive time – heading southwest through Colorado, south to the Grand Canyon, east through New Mexico and Texas, and finally north again to home – on one of our greatest family vacations. During the entire trip, we watched only three movies. Yes, just three. How did we do this? By listening to great audio books. Together we listened to and memorized poems (from Andrew Pudewa's Institute for Excellence in Writing poetry program), sang songs, prayed, and enjoyed many stories. The younger children were introduced to Paddington Bear, Curious George, and Corduroy. All of us solved mysteries with the Hardy boys and Nancy Drew, held our breath as the Baudelaire children battled their evil uncle in *A Series of Unfortunate Events*, and became engrossed in the adventures of Jonathan Park (learning more about creation science than we ever knew existed). The sharing together of great audio books added immeasurably to the enjoyment and value of this trip, which we look back on as one truly blessed by God.

Since that time, we've driven to the east coast, the Smoky Mountains,

5 STEPS TO SUCCESSFUL HOME SCHOOLING

South Dakota, Wyoming, Florida, and many trips to Wisconsin. Whenever and wherever we go, we make sure to pack great audio books for the journey. As a family, we've enjoyed *The Adventures of Tom Sawyer, Just So Stories, Sherlock Holmes, The Secret Garden, The Railway Children, Little Lord Fauntleroy, Anastasia Krupnik, Romana Quimby, Farmer Boy, Glory Stories* (audio stories about the lives of saints), *Whittington*, and many, many others on audio CD. It has been such a blessing to share these stories with our children. When we travel, not only do we remember and enjoy our trips, but also the stories we listened to together.

When the kids were younger, the announcement that we'd be listening to a new audio book was greeted by cheers and lively opinions about its selection. Once they hit the teen years, however, their enthusiasm has not been as strong. Finding books that are appropriate and enjoyable for all age levels in our family takes some diligence, planning, and cheerleading. It's been necessary to limit 'electronics time' (in the home and in the car) with iPods and handheld gaming devices, and we've had to work harder to develop anticipation for each new book session.

At home, we continue to read aloud to all of the children. Our younger children and I read out loud during the school day and also at night. Finding time to read with our busy high school age children has become more challenging, but we manage to fit it in somehow most weeks. Reading aloud has been a great way to stay connected with our teens and initiate conversations that otherwise might not take place.

Our family treasures the time we spend reading together, and we laugh often at the many memories we have shared through books. Indeed, a fun memory is of the time when we were reading one of our all time favorite books, *Where the Red Fern Grows*. We were toward the end of the story when tragedy struck. Upon reading this pitiful drama, I began crying too hard to continue, so my oldest daughter took over. But, she too, began crying over the tragic words.

STEP 3: READ QUALITY LITERATURE

Finally, my son (who was ten years old at the time), took the book from us emotional women and finished the chapter for us. We all laugh at that memory today and still agree that it is an excellent book.

Reading can strengthen one's faith

Reading can also help grow and develop faith – your children's and your own. Certainly, memorizing the gifts of the Holy Spirit, the Ten Commandments, the prayers of the rosary, and the four marks of the church are important. Equally important, however, is learning about how people put the truths of our faith into action. Reading about the humility of St. Therese of Lisieux, the service of Blessed Mother Teresa to the poor, and the integrity and fidelity of St. Thomas More shows us what faith in action looks like. The lives of these and other holy people teach us all how to pray, serve, love, and grow in faith.

Spiritual reading is important for adults as well as children. Matthew Kelly, in his book *Rediscover Catholicism*, describes its value in this way,

> "Books change our lives. Most people can identify a book that has marked a life-changing period in their lives. It was probably a book that said just the right thing at just the right time. They may have been just words on a page, but they came to life for you, and in you, and because of them you will never again be the same. It is true, books change our lives. What we read today walks and talks with us tomorrow. . . .The goal of spiritual reading is to ignite the soul with a desire to grow in virtue and thus become the best-version-of-oneself."

So what spiritual books should you read with your children? Above all, we should read the Bible. There is also St. Joseph's Baltimore Catechism, which proclaims the fundamental principles of the Catholic faith. In addition, there are wonderful books about saints and other men and women who strived to live out their faith.

53

5 STEPS TO SUCCESSFUL HOME SCHOOLING

Likewise, there are excellent Christian works of fiction populated with characters that both succeed and fail in their Christian walk. Through these readings, children learn about the 'heroes' of our Catholic faith. Your children will experience vicariously situations in which Christian virtues are tested and they will see how characters (both fictional and real) respond to these challenges.

CHOOSE QUALITY READING MATERIAL

By now, you probably agree that teaching your children to read, encouraging them to pore over great books, reading aloud with them, and reading yourself can provide immeasurable value to your family. The key, however, to accessing the many advantages offered by reading is to make good book choices.

Have you ever heard someone say, "Well, it doesn't matter what my child is reading, as long as they are reading; that's all that's important." What a sad and misguided statement this is! That's like saying, "It doesn't matter what my child is eating, I'm just glad he's eating." How ridiculous! Anyone with even the smallest amount of common sense can tell you that a steady diet of jelly donuts, candy, and fast food leads to inferior growth development and poor health. It's the same with the books that we read. A steady diet of poorly written material filled with slang, poor grammar, and inappropriate story lines can hinder the mental growth and character development of your child.

If you introduce your children to rich literature, and offer this on a regular basis, they will grow to desire this quality of writing and choose it over other options because they will recognize the difference. Remember, your children will realize the highest benefits of reading only if you read them great literature and give them access to excellent books to read on their own. I once met a woman at a seminar who called herself a book snob, saying that

54

STEP 3: READ QUALITY LITERATURE

there are so many good books available that she refuses to waste her time on those that are mediocre or poorly written. At the time, I didn't understand. Now, nearly a decade later, I get it, and have also become a literature snob. Through home schooling, I've been introduced to a world of rich literature, more great books than could possibly be read in a lifetime. With such an abundance of interesting, exciting, wonderful, and transformative books available to all ages; reading books of lesser quality (with or without my children) seems a senseless waste of time. Hence, I've become very particular about the books I choose to read for myself and my children. They must be high quality indeed to be selected among such bounty!

What books are considered quality? What books should we be reading to our children? A full list of excellent reading material is much too long to include in this book. There are, however, many wonderful books dedicated to listing and describing great literature choices for children and teens. They are excellent resources for parents and educators and I strongly encourage you to own one or more of them. Four books I recommend are:

1. *Honey for the Child's Heart* by Gladys Hunt
2. *Honey for the Teen's Heart* by Gladys Hunt
3. *Turning the Pages of Time: A Guide to American History through Literature*. This pamphlet is compiled by Kathy Keller
4. *Books Children Love* by Elizabeth Wilson

Each of these books provides wonderful lists and descriptions of great literature (with appropriate age ranges) for children. I access these lists continually as my children age or we encounter different units in our curriculum.

For those of you just beginning to home educate your children, or for those who are looking for a quick list of recommended books for children and adults, our family's 'Top Ten' books for different age groups are listed on the following pages. These books are enjoyable and worth reading whether or not you are home schooling, but in no

55

5 STEPS TO SUCCESSFUL HOME SCHOOLING

way do they represent a comprehensive reading guide for curriculum planning. For that purpose, please read Laura Berquist's *Designing Your Own Curriculum: A Guide to Catholic Home Education* or Susan Wise Bauer's *The Well Trained Mind: A Guide to Classical Education at Home*. These guides provide a comprehensive curriculum reading list for each grade and subject. Other home school programs such as Seton Home School or Mother of Divine Grace, also provide thorough lists of reading material for every grade and subject. Contact information for these resources can be found in the Appendix of this book.

The books I have listed on the following pages are the books that our family most often suggests and the ones enjoyed by other people we know. They are recommended for all children as a starting point or introduction to the wonderful world of great literature. I hope your family will enjoy them as much as we have.

Preschool

1. *The Carrot Seed* by Ruth Krauss
2. *The Little Drummer Boy* by Ezra Jack Keats
3. *Whistle for Willie* by Ezra Jack Keats
4. *Little Bear* by Else Minarik
5. *Caps for Sale* by Esphyr Slobodkina
6. *Cowboy Small* by Lois Lenski (and other "small" books by this author)
7. *Click, Clack, Moo Cows That Type* by Doreen Cronin
8. *The Giving Tree* by Shel Silverstein
9. *Fireman Small* by Wong Herbert Yee
10. *Goodnight Moon* by Margaret Wise Brown

Grades K-2

1. *Flicka, Ricka, and Dicka* series by Maj Lindman
2. *Ox-Cart Man* by Donald Hall
3. *The Lady of Guadalupe* by Tomie de Paola (and other books by this author)

STEP 3: READ QUALITY LITERATURE

4. *Adventures of Frog and Toad* by Arnold Lobel
5. *A New Coat for Anna* by Harriet Ziefert and Anita Lobel
6. *Billy and Blaze* series by C.W. Anderson
7. *The Magic Treehouse* series by Mary Pope Osborne
8. *The Boxcar Children* series by Gertrude Chandler Warner
9. *The Courage of Sarah Noble* by Alice Dalgliesh
10. *Ramona Quimby*, Age 8 by Beverly Cleary

Grades 3-4

1. *Sarah Plain and Tall* by Patricia MacLachlan
2. *Little House on the Prairie* books by Laura Ingalls Wilder
3. *Ginger Pye* by Eleanor Estes (and other books by this author)
4. *Betsy Tacy* series by Maud Hart Lovelace
5. *Homer Price* by Robert McClosky
6. *Little Lord Fauntleroy* by Frances Hodgson Burnett
7. *Pollyanna* by Eleanor H. Porter
8. *Charlotte's Web* by E.B. White
9. *The Orphans Find A Home: A St. Frances Xavier Cabrini Story* by Joan Stromberg
10. *The Mitchells: Five for Victory* by Hilda van Stockum

Grades 5-6

1. *The Lion the Witch and the Wardrobe* series by C.S. Lewis
2. *Plain Girl* by Virginia Sorensen
3. *The Secret Garden* by Frances Hodgson Burnett (the BBC audio dramatization at the library is worth listening to!)
4. *The Sign of the Beaver* by Elizabeth George Speare
5. *Shades of Gray* by Carolyn Reeder (great Civil War story!)
6. *Number the Stars* by Lois Lowry
7. *The Best/Worst Christmas Pageant Ever* by Barbara Robinson
8. *All of a Kind Family* by Sydney Taylor
9. *The Cure of Ars* by Milton Lomask
10. *Bud, Not Buddy* by Christopher Paul Curtis

5 STEPS TO SUCCESSFUL HOME SCHOOLING

Grades 7-9

1. *My Louisiana Sky* by Kimberly Willis Holt
2. *Across Five Aprils* by Irene Hunt
3. *Where the Red Fern Grows* by Wilson Rawls
4. *The Hiding Place* by Corrie ten Boom
5. *The Hobbit and The Lord of the Rings Trilogy* by J.R.R. Tolkien
6. *Laddie* by Gene Stratton-Porter (and other books by this author)
7. *Julie of the Wolves* by Jean Craighead George
8. *Island of the Blue Dolphins* by Scott O'Dell
9. *Anne of Green Gables* by Lucy Maud Montgomery
10. *Roll of Thunder Hear My Cry* by Mildred D. Taylor

Grades 10-12

1. *The Robe* by Lloyd Douglas
2. *Left to Tell* by Immaculée Ilibagiza
3. *What Ever Happened to Penny Candy* by Richard J. Maybury
4. *The Rhythm of Life* by Matthew Kelly
5. *To Kill A Mockingbird* by Harper Lee
6. *Anne Frank: The Diary of a Young Girl*
7. *Le Morte d'Arthur: King Arthur and the Legend of the Round Table* by Sir Thomas Malory
8. *The Ballad of the White Horse* by G.K. Chesterton (and other books by this author)
9. *Pride and Prejudice* by Jane Austen
10. *The Screwtape Letters* and *Mere Christianity* by C.S. Lewis

Adults

1. *The Bible.* (In addition to daily Scripture reading and prayer, I strongly recommend Bible study programs by Jeff Cavins. These Bible studies will enhance your understanding of Scripture)
2. *Designing Your Own Classical Curriculum: A Guide to Catholic Home Education* by Laura Berquist
3. *The Well-Trained Mind: A Guide to Classical Education at Home* by Susan Wise Bauer and Jessie Wise

STEP 3: READ QUALITY LITERATURE

4. *Honey for the Child's Heart* by Gladys Hunt
5. *For the Children's Sake: Foundations of Education for Home and School* by Susan Schaeffer Macaulay
6. *A Mother's Rule of Life: How to Bring Order to Your Home and Peace to Your Soul* by Holly Pierlot
7. *The Hawk and the Dove Trilogy* by Penelope Wilcock
8. *The Lamb's Supper* by Dr. Scott Hahn
9. *Parenting With Love and Logic* and *Parenting Teens With Love and Logic* by Foster Cline, M.D. and Jim Fay
10. *The Story of a Soul: The Autobiography of St. Therese of Lisieux* translation by John Clarke, O.C.D.
11. Read all of the books listed above for children and adults!

ESTABLISH GOOD READING HABITS

Not all children (even my own) enjoy reading. There are some who read avidly and others who do it only because they have to. Some people simply find reading more enjoyable than others. The important point, however, is to continue trying! I read aloud more often with my reluctant readers than with the ones who like to read on their own. I also spend a great deal of time choosing books and magazine articles that might be of interest to them. My son does not enjoy reading. Over the years, I have attended many literature conferences that discuss great books for boys, pored over lists of recommended reading, and talked with other parents of boys, always seeking more book choices. Often I pre-read the recommended books in a further attempt to determine if my son will like them. This takes a lot of energy and effort, but the effort has been worthwhile. Despite his dislike of reading, my son is a well-read young man. His main strengths lie in the area of mathematics, but he is very articulate and can read and write well.

Whether you have a child who is a book worm or a reluctant reader, you can encourage reading in your family by following these four steps:

5 Steps to Successful Home Schooling

Model this behavior by reading

The most important step in encouraging your children to read is to be a reader yourself. If you want your children to read the Bible when they are adults, they should see you reading your Bible. They must see you reading quality newspapers and magazines if you want them to be up on current events when they grow up. If you want your children to read classics, spiritual books, or good books for entertainment as adults, they should see you doing the same daily. That's right, daily. Your children will model the behavior they see, so if you want them to be life-long learners, then you must model that behavior for them.

That doesn't mean you need to spend four hours a day reading. A minimum of fifteen minutes of daily reading doesn't seem unreasonable, though. The benefits gained from this quarter hour of reading can be tremendous. Your brain, just like your muscles, needs regular exercise, and reading quality literature is an excellent way to keep your mind at the top of its game. To compound the benefits of daily reading, share facts or discuss ideas that you encounter with your spouse and children. This simple act will greatly encourage your children to becoming life-long readers themselves.

Make reading enjoyable

One of the fastest ways to kill any enjoyment a child gets from reading is to assign a book report. That's not to say that a book report never needs to be written. Indeed, there is value in doing so. However, if you want reading to be an activity that your children enjoy and look forward to, do everything you can to keep it enjoyable. How can you do this?

First, never use reading as a form of discipline. If your child misbehaves and requires a time out, do not allow them to read during this time out. This helps them to understand that reading is

STEP 3: READ QUALITY LITERATURE

a privilege that can be lost with misbehavior. Instead, use reading as a reward. For example, if your children have worked particularly hard during the school day study session, offer them an extra fifteen minutes or half hour of reading time later in the day or the following day.

Second, offer many reading choices to your children. Without question, there will be some books assigned as part of your curriculum. Most, but not all of these books, will be enjoyable to your children. We all have different tastes when it comes to literature. Some children prefer fantasy while others choose mystery and still others like biographies. Assigned curricular books must be read by all, but in addition to assigned reading, offer your children a wide variety of quality reading choices to select for enjoyment. Books make excellent gifts! Have them make lists of books that they want to read, and consider making these lists available to gift-giving relatives for birthdays and Christmas. And don't forget the library, an excellent resource that provides access to countless quality books at no cost.

Finally, set an ambience for reading. One of my children loves to eat popcorn. Every now and then, when a half hour of reading time is announced, we'll pop some corn to munch on while reading. (However, don't get into the habit of snacking every time you read, or you'll not only increase your knowledge, but your waistline as well!) In the winter, light a fire and cuddle up on the couch for reading time. During the spring and summer months, take your books outside and enjoy them while lying in a hammock or on a blanket in the grass. Reading in a tent under the table or in the backyard can add fun to this activity, as does reading in or under a child's own bed, or all snuggled up together in the parents' bed.

Schedule reading time and limit screen time

Another way to encourage your child to become a reader is to schedule reading time every day. If you home school, this is easy to

61

do by simply incorporating reading time into your daily schedule. However, during the summer months, or for families whose children attend regular school, this can be more difficult. In the summer, have your children spend between half an hour and one hour reading every day. If there's no time during the day, have them do it in the evening. This 'down time' can be just what's needed for relaxation during the hectic summer time. If scheduled reading time isn't a habit for your children, they may initially balk at the idea. However, if you stick with it, they will get accustomed to it and most likely will come to enjoy it!

In addition to scheduling reading, it is important to set boundaries around your children's 'screen time'. Whether it's the computer, handheld games, electronic television games, music devices, or cell phones, our children need time limits for using them. These devices can be great fun and very educational, however, overuse can be detrimental and take away from other beneficial forms of entertainment (including reading). It's easy to set a time limit. It can be difficult, however, to enforce it. This takes vigilance, patience, and effort. Some helpful strategies include setting the timer, giving heads-up notice that a time limit will soon be up, and inviting participation in a game or activity with you once they have reached their limit.

Creating a home in which reading is important takes some work. The benefits, however, are well worth the effort. Although you need to be intentional about raising your children to be life-long readers, this endeavor will not feel like drudgery. In fact, it will bring many hours of enjoyment and wonder to you and your family for years to come!

A Word About Struggling Readers

Some of you reading this chapter may think that reading is great – for those who have children who can read well. But, for children who struggle to read, this activity can be far from enjoyable – it can be

STEP 3: READ QUALITY LITERATURE

grueling. For those of you with children who struggle to read, I have two recommendations:

First, be patient, persistent, and observant. Not all children learn to read at the age of 5 years, or 6 years, or 9 years. If your child is in the lower elementary grades, and is struggling to read, don't sound the alarms quite yet. Be patient with your child. Help them to read their assignments, easy reader books, and easy poems. In addition, provide great literature to them in the form of audio books. A child's ability (or inability) to read is rarely a reflection of their intelligence, and their ability to comprehend an audio book written for their grade level (or even a grade above their level) is often assured. Continue working with them through their course work, patiently understanding that your assistance will be necessary for them to read directions and complete assignments. If you are the parent of a struggling reader, you will likely need to adjust your schedule and priorities to be able to spend more time with that child. While working with them, be observant. Do they get headaches often? Do they complain of blurry vision or double vision? Do they struggle with anything other than reading, for example handwriting, following basic instructions, or simple math facts? Do they have any physical issues that might be contributing to their reading struggles such as poor nutrition, a tendency toward ADHD, did they require speech therapy as a toddler, or do they have any special needs?

Of my five children, two of them learned to read with virtually no effort at all. The other three have struggled. My oldest daughter had great difficulty with reading until the fourth grade. During the early elementary years, we continued with her course work, I assisted her with all assignments, and I continued to read great literature aloud. In the fourth grade, I could almost see the light bulb go off in her brain. Something clicked and her reading ability soared. This daughter, who is now in high school, is my most prolific reader. When my fourth child followed the same pattern, I did not worry about her reading struggles early on. However, in fourth grade, the light bulb did not go off for her. She continued to struggle painfully while I began to

63

worry. When no improvements were made during the fourth grade, I sought out help and testing for my daughter. As a result of the testing, we learned that she has dyslexia.

My second recommendation is to seek assistance. For those of you with children who struggle to read, the best thing you can do for your child is to continue to provide excellent literature to them in the form of audio books and seek out help. A great place to begin to look for help is the Home School Legal Defense Association's website. (Listed in Chapter 5). This organization has a staff trained in working with families who have children with special needs – including dyslexia. Through their help, I was able to find excellent books for me (to help me learn about dyslexia in children), and resources to use with my child. The gains my daughter has made by having access to resources and help has been tremendous. My daughter is an intelligent child (as were Leonardo DaVinci, Albert Einstein, and Henry Ford – all of whom were dyslexic). She can learn, but she learns differently from my other children. If I provide the material in a format that meets her learning style, she absorbs it readily. Fortunately, there are many resources available for educators and students who struggle with reading. My daughter may never find reading to be easy, but through audio books, technology, and resources, she will be able to learn all of her subjects, and have wonderful exposure to excellent literature. Your struggling reader, too, can achieve success with the right tools and support. See Chapter 5 for additional information.

STEP 3:
READ QUALITY LITERATURE

1. Believe in the value of reading.

2. Choose quality reading material.

3. Establish good reading habits.

    a. Model this behavior by reading yourself every day.

    b. Read aloud to your children and/or schedule independent reading time.

    c. Make reading as enjoyable as possible.

    d. Limit screen time.

4. Seek out help and/or resources for the struggling reader.

Step 4: Get Organized

"In the beginning, when God created the heavens and the earth, the earth was a formless wasteland, and darkness covered the abyss, while a mighty wind swept over the waters. Then God said, "Let there be light," and there was light. . . Then God said, "Let there be a dome in the middle of the waters, to separate one body of water from another." And so it happened. . . Then God said, "Let the water under the sky be gathered into a single basin, so that dry land may appear." . . . Then God said, "Let the earth bring forth vegetation . . ." Then God said, "Let there be lights in the dome of the sky, to separate day from night. dLet them mark the fixed times, the days and the years . . ." Then God said, "Let the water teem with an abundance of living creatures, and on the earth let birds fly. . ." Then God said, "Let the earth bring forth all kinds of living creatures. . ." Thus the heavens and the earth and all their array were completed."
(Genesis 1:1-2:1)

Our God is a God of order, not chaos. The Bible shows clearly that God has always had a plan for His people, including us today. Our goal, as Christians, is to discern God's will for us, and live according to this plan. For some of us, His plan includes home schooling our children.

5 STEPS TO SUCCESSFUL HOME SCHOOLING

Successful home education requires much self discipline. Already we've discussed the importance of: regular prayer; identification of a mission and goals for your family as a whole and for each individual; and the habit of reading. A fourth important step of any home educator is that of being organized. Simply being a parent and running a household takes a fair amount of organization. Shopping for groceries, making meals, paying bills, sorting laundry, cleaning bathrooms, planning birthday parties, carpooling to sporting practices, scheduling and keeping appointments with doctors, dentists, orthodontists, and barbers, are just a few of the things that most parents do on a regular basis. Home educators must do all of the aforementioned tasks and, in addition, carry out curriculum research, selection, and planning; teach each child his or her lessons; correct homework; write and review mission statements; administer standardized testing; attend conferences; read; pray; complete required school district paperwork; prepare transcripts; plan field trips and other school related activities; etc. Indeed, the only way to get it all completed, on time, is to get organized.

To get organized, focus on these three important areas of life: 1) your priorities – the big picture; 2) your monthly calendar; and 3) your daily routine.

SET YOUR PRIORITIES

Before deciding if you should schedule math for ten o'clock on Tuesday mornings and sign up for Saturday afternoon swim lessons, take a look at the big picture. If you've written a mission statement (as recommended in Step 2), review the values and goals you identified during that process. Decide which are of highest priority, and schedule activities related to those things *first*.

Our former pastor, Fr. Arnold Weber, OSB often stated that one's priorities should be: God, spouse, family, work – in that order. He

STEP 4: GET ORGANIZED

then went on to say that the priorities we actually live by can be identified by simply looking at our calendars and our checkbook. This statement made me pause and reflect. I know what I tell myself and others about my priorities, but did I really give those items the time and attention that they deserved?

Do you consider your faith life to be a priority? If so, do your calendars and finances reflect this belief? Closely examine your calendar and checkbook now to discover if your relationship with God, which should hold top priority, is lacking. So far this book has identified the importance of prayer (Step 1) and spiritual reading (Step 3) in daily life. Does your daily planner indicate time set aside for these and other worthy spiritual pursuits (such as Bible study and family faith formation) that show God truly holds a place of honor and intention? Answer this question before deciding whether or not to sign your child up for the travel soccer program or the debate club. Reflect upon this most significant big picture before adding anything else to your calendar. In addition, closely examine your finances. Do you give to the Church and to those in need? Are you being a good steward with what God has given you? Is there room for improvement? If so, identify your improvement plan before adding additional expenses to your budget.

According to Fr. Weber, after your relationship with God comes your relationship with your spouse. Most people would agree that their marriages are important, yet a close look at their calendars might reveal that little time is invested in their relationship as a couple. After balancing work, volunteer activities, social engagements, household responsibilities, and keeping up with the children and their activities, many couples are too exhausted to expend even a small amount of time for daily conversation. If your marriage is truly important, however, you must be intentional about maintaining it. Schedule on a regular basis time to spend together doing something you both enjoy, even if it means occasionally saying no to other invitations and activities. Plan a weekly (or biweekly or monthly) date night. Set aside thirty minutes after dinner each night to converse and reconnect. Go away for a night or a weekend once or twice a year. Keeping your marriage a priority takes creativity and sacrifice, but it is worth the effort.

Third on the list of big picture priorities are children and/or extended family. Home educators are fortunate to be able to spend many hours each and every day with their children. Spending such quantity and quality time with my children, learning right along with them, day after day, year after year, has certainly blessed me immensely. But be wise about how your home school and/or family time is spent; that is, be careful and conscious when planning activities in which your children participate. Before making any specific plan (educational or other), be sure to review your mission statement. Assess each of your children individually, considering his or her personal needs and your goals for him or her. Look at the gifts and interests of each as well as areas in which growth is needed. Finally, consider the needs of the family as a whole. If there's a new baby or you're moving houses, everyone might need to decrease the number of outside activities in which they participate for a while as the family adjusts to its new member or living situation. On the other hand, this may be the time or season when it's both desirable and possible for you and your children to be involved in multiple outside activities. Keep in mind, though, that just because your neighbor's children are each involved in a dozen activities does not mean that same number and type of activities are appropriate for yours. Activities can be good, but as the saying goes, 'too much of a good thing' can be detrimental to everyone.

As a home educator, be sure to remember that your children should rank third in priority, behind your relationships with God and spouse. If there is any danger for home educators (in the area of priorities) it is that they have a tendency to place the children above their relationship with God and their spouse. Because home schooling demands so much time and energy, it is easy to let your relationship with God and your spouse take a back seat. To prevent this from happening, be organized and purposeful in planning for your faith

STEP 4: GET ORGANIZED

development and marriage enrichment. My friend Jennifer, a ten year home schooling veteran, told me that she schedules a 20-30 minute nap for herself each afternoon to make certain that she has energy to converse with her husband when he gets home later in the day! Not everyone needs a daytime nap, but we all must recognize the importance of making time for our highest priorities. Home schooling, coupled with numerous activities for the children, has a way of sneaking in and robbing you of time and energy from many other things in life. No matter how noble these pursuits are, do not let them usurp your top priorities, namely God and your spouse.

Finally, the fourth priority in the big picture is work. Without question, work is necessary and a vital part of life. However, if the amount of time or energy you or your spouse spend on work significantly impacts your family in a negative way, then a conversation needs to take place to see if adjustments can be made. Something to consider when reviewing your family's work life is the possibility of starting a family business and/or involving your home schooled children in your work. Home schooling families who have successfully started family businesses use them as a training ground for the children to acquire marketable real life workplace skills. Hands-on education is often the best education, and what better way to offer this type of learning than through a family business?

LOOK AT YOUR MONTHLY CALENDAR

Once you've looked at the big picture, the next step in getting organized is to focus on the monthly calendar. If you do not have a central calendar on which all family appointments and activities are written (or one you've created on the computer), I encourage you to do so. In either case, you might like to color code the appointments and activities of each family member. For example, write all of your appointments in blue and your spouse's in red. Make little Billy's green and daughter Sally's orange. You get the idea. Whether you color code your calendar entries or not, the most important factor in staying organized is that you keep one family calendar accessible in a central location.

As a home schooling parent, in planning your monthly calendar, be aware of these factors that may disrupt your daily routine:

Scheduling too many outside engagements during the school hours

Although it's easy and tempting to schedule piano lessons, doctor appointments, and other important meetings in prime daytime hours, having to leave for these engagements can disrupt the day's routine and make it difficult to accomplish necessary school work. I've learned not to schedule any lessons or appointments before 2:00 pm, which gives us the entire morning, the noon hour, and a chunk of time after lunch to get through our day's school work.

Signing up to participate in too many outside classes

Home school classes that are offered outside your home can be very worthwhile. There are many available that offer excellent tutors or teachers who share wonderful knowledge in a variety of subject areas. It's also fun for your children to participate in 'classroom' experiences with other home schooled youth. Carefully consider how many classes you choose to join, however, recognizing that they will interrupt your home school days, and the fewer interruptions to your daily routine the better.

One family I know begins their school day at 7:00am with morning devotions and works diligently until noon. They use the afternoon hours for music lessons, classes, appointments, and working on their home business. Another family schedules all of their outside classes, appointments, and lessons on the same day of the week. They run from sun up till sun down on that day, but stick to their school routine at home the other days of the week. Other families enroll in on-line classes and limit the number of outside classes they must run out to attend. Many excellent Catholic on-line programs exist, some of which are listed in the appendix of this book.

Each year we adjust our monthly and daily schedules based upon the current needs of our children and the availability of desired classes. Occasionally, even though it's not ideal, we take some morning classes, and there have been times when we have had to schedule appointments during the school day. The more we can maintain a daily routine, however, the more successful we are in getting through our planned work.

LOOK AT YOUR DAILY SCHEDULE

This leads to the last area of schedule organization - the daily schedule. Having a daily routine should be a high priority for anyone choosing to educate their children at home. Having a schedule helps us to be more productive and efficient with our time. In addition, children thrive when following a routine appropriate for their ages, stages, and abilities. They learn to anticipate what will be happening each day and work securely and confidently throughout the day.

The first year we home schooled our children, I read a book called *Managers of Their Homes: A Practical Guide to Daily Scheduling for Christian Homeschool Families* by Steven and Teri Maxwell. This book was a wonderful resource for me. After reading the book, talking with other home school parents, and looking at the goals we had for each child, I prepared a detailed daily schedule (divided into fifteen minute increments) for each of our children. The first month after this went smoothly, pretty much according to schedule, with a few minor adjustments. Then during the second month, I noticed my stress level rising every time an unplanned event (good or bad) occurred to make us deviate from the schedule. Every unannounced visitor or phone call, every unexpected invitation or opportunity, every illness or injury, caused extra stress and tension simply because

5 STEPS TO SUCCESSFUL HOME SCHOOLING

they interfered with the schedule, which I had unintentionally allowed to become the ruler of our home rather than the servant guide.

Fortunately, at the next meeting of my wonderful home school support group, I mentioned how stressed and bothered I was feeling if we didn't stay on task and accomplish all the assigned work according to schedule. One wise group member reminded me that our schedules are meant to help us create a *routine*, not an inflexible timed task list. Another wise woman from the group noted that our mission statements should help direct our schedule. One of the benefits to home schooling is that our schedules can be flexible. She suggested that, occasionally taking time to make a meal for a needy neighbor, visiting a relative who is sick or lonely, or simply pausing to watch the birds on the feeder helps to develop character and a love for learning that no lesson plan can provide. What wisdom I gained from them!

We still have schedules for each child and each day of the week. Indeed, home schooling multiple children requires a certain amount of time management to ensure that everyone stays as productive as possible (for example, as you work with one child on math, the others are busy working independently on something else). However, we now use these schedules as flexible guides, with time built in for necessary modification. I no longer fret if it takes 45 minutes, (instead of the planned 30 minutes), for my child to understand his or her math lesson on fractions.

In deciding how to organize your home school day, create a plan that will work well for you and your children. I have created a schedule for each of my children for every day of the week. I have printed out each schedule and placed them in a clear, page protector in the child's three-ring schedule binder. Each day, as they complete a task, they use a dry-erase marker to cross off each subject. Using the page protectors and dry erase markers allows us to re-use the schedules week after week.

STEP 4: GET ORGANIZED

Some children, especially younger children, those who are new to home schooling, or those with learning disabilities, may need you to prompt them to move from subject to subject or activity to activity throughout the day. Others, typically middle school and high school age children, will do well in completing subjects and activities on their own according to the schedule. Still others may benefit from having the freedom to choose the order in which they complete their daily assignments. As the teacher, you also may have preferences as to how your home school schedules are followed. Consider your own and your children's unique needs and preferences, then build and use your daily schedules accordingly.

Following, I have listed two examples of schedules that we have used for our children. In the Appendix, additional schedules and schedule templates are provided. The most common schedule we have used is the spreadsheet schedule. This type of schedule works well for my personality and the number of children we currently school at home. However, we have also used a more flexible format which is shown on the page following the spreadsheets.

5 Steps to Successful Home Schooling

Monday home school schedule (no outside classes on this day)

	Child #1	Child #2	Child #3	Child #4
8:15-8:45	Mom works on	her Bible study.	Kids make beds,	clean rooms,teeth
9:00	Prayer	Prayer	Prayer	Prayer
9:30	math	grammar	cursive & poetry	penmanship & chores
10:00	Spanish	math	math w/mom	math w/mom
10:30	geography then snack	reading comp & snack	grammar w/mom	piano & snack
11:00	grammar	piano & chores	snack & piano	grammar w/mom
11:30	spelling & chores	Spanish & poetry	violin	poetry
12:00	lunch	lunch	lunch	lunch
12:30	free	free	free	free
1:00	history	history	history	history
1:30	public speaking class homework	writing class homework	writing class homework	exercise
2:00	read	read	read	read
2:30	science	science	reading comp.	Explode the Code
3:00	mom reads	mom reads	mom reads	mom reads
3:30	research writing/essay class homework	geography	exercise	
4:00	flute	exercise		
4:30	exercise			
5:00		leave at 5:15 for dance		
evening		Dance class		

STEP 4: GET ORGANIZED

Tuesday home school schedule (outside classes scheduled in the morning)

	Child #1	Child #2	Child #3	Child #4
8:30	Leave for classes	Leave for classes	Leave for classes	Leave for classes
9:00	Research writing/essay class	Art class	Art class	Science class
9:30	Writing class	Art class	Art class	Science class
10:00	Science class	Spanish class	Essay writing class	Art class
10:30	Science class	Spanish class	Essay writing class	Art class
11:00	Public speaking class	Science class	Science class	Writing class
11:30	Public speaking class	Science class	Science class	Writing class
12:00	Drive home	drive home	drive home	drive home
12:30	Lunch	Lunch	Lunch	Lunch
1:00	math	piano	math w/mom	math w/mom
1:30	Spanish	piano & geography	piano & poetry	geography
2:00	Science	math	geography	piano & poetry
2:30	religion workbook	Spanish & chores	Cursive writing & chores	penmanship & chores
3:00	poetry & chores	Religion workbook	violin	free
3:30	spelling	poetry		
4:00	flute			
4:30				
5:00			violin lesson	
evening				

77

5 STEPS TO SUCCESSFUL HOME SCHOOLING

Child #1 (Middle School Age) Flexible Monday Schedule

9:00 am　　　　　　**Prayer**

9:30-11:00　　　　　**Complete the following in any order**
Math
Flute practice
Spelling
Science home work

11:00 – 12:30　　　　**Now complete these in any order**
Snack/Play with dog
Grammar
Research paper and essay writing class
homework

12:30-1:30　　　　　**Lunch**

1:30-3:00　　　　　　**Complete these in any order**
Read for 30 minutes
Public speaking class homework
Spanish homework
Religion/Geography

3:00　　　　　　　　**Mom reads**

3:30　　　　　　　　Complete any work that did not get done

STEP 4: GET ORGANIZED

You will notice on the spreadsheet schedules included in this book that most days include a full hour lunch break. Rarely does it take us that long to eat our sandwiches or leftovers. However, we all benefit from a 'recess.' In addition, if we've run overtime on our morning schedule for some reason – a child needing extra help on a lesson, an important phone call that needs to be made or taken, an unexpected visitor briefly stops by – we don't worry about falling behind because, if necessary, our lunch break can be shortened just a bit. After lunch, the children have time to go outside (weather permitting), play with indoor games and toys, or read leisurely. In addition, I have a chance to check voicemail and e-mails and respond to any urgent messages. This free time re-charges everyone's batteries for the second part of our day.

Notice also that our schedules are broken down into half hour time blocks. This allows for some 'time fidgeting.' For example, rarely does it take a full 30 minutes for any child to accomplish some of their activities (such as snack/play with the dog, or their penmanship practice). However, the extra time built in for this activity may be used to make up for extra time taken in other areas.

Following the spreadsheet examples is a model of a schedule that we have used from time to time for some of our children as a break from the typical, more precise format. This schedule allows the children to select the order in which they complete a specific set of activities within a certain time frame. For example, from 9:30am to 11:00am, one child may choose in which order they complete math, music practice, handwriting and reading. Another child, during that same time slot, may choose in which order they complete grammar, math, poetry, and reading comprehension. All their required tasks must be completed within the designated time frame, but the sequence of completion is up to the child. The same process occurs again, then, beginning at 11:00am, when the child works on a different set of subjects in his or her preferred sequence.

Some families that we know simply assign their children the required

79

5 STEPS TO SUCCESSFUL HOME SCHOOLING

work for the day or the week and allow them to complete it all according to their own schedules. This system works best with older (high school) children, but the process toward such independence should begin in middle school and gradually be expanded as the children mature. Giving children the opportunity to help plan their own schedules and budget their own time to complete assignments can be highly educational. Remember, though, that mastering these disciplines is almost always a gradual process.

Because of the age ranges within my family (high school down to elementary school), and the amount of time I must still spend with each child, a more specific time schedule works best for us right now. We have realized, however, that schedules change from semester to semester, or year to year, and what works best one year may be different the following year. Remember, also, that every family is unique, so create the kind of schedule that works best for your situation, whatever that is right now.

Most important of all, remember that your schedule serves as a guide to help ensure that you're covering all of the subjects for all of the children and that when you work with one child individually, the rest have independent work to keep them busy. As the wise woman from my home school support group stated, the value of a schedule comes from the routine it establishes for you to follow rather than from a strict adherence to arbitrary times for starting each and every activity throughout the day.

Getting and staying organized really is one of the most important challenges you will face as a home educator. It takes effort and discipline to identify priorities in your life, make time for them, and schedule your monthly, weekly, and daily activities around them. Doing so, however, will help you achieve a greater level of success in your home schooling. In addition, you will be modeling a valuable behavior for your children. Remember, if you want them to pray as adults, you need to pray yourself. If you want them to be readers, you must be reading yourself. Likewise, if you want your children

STEP 4: GET ORGANIZED

to be organized adults, you must make every effort to be organized yourself now. You'll be training your children in a discipline that will serve them well throughout life.

KEEP STUDY MATERIALS AND AREA NEAT

Finally, the last area of organization that will help to facilitate your home school success is your home itself. This book is not going to give you a process for organizing your house and keeping it that way. It won't offer tips on cleaning out your closets or streamlining your kitchen. It simply emphasizes that maintaining some order in your home can increase your level of success in home education.

A permanently tidy home may be a stretch, depending on the number and ages of your children, but do the best you can to keep your home school materials as orderly as possible. It is helpful if you have a specific area or room to store all of your curriculum materials, documents, and books.

Before our basement was finished, we did not have a room in which we could store all of our home school materials. Most of our schooling was done at the kitchen table. During those years, the children and I each had a plastic milk crate in which we stored all of our curriculum and teaching materials. When we were schooling, the kids placed their milk crates on the floor next to their chairs at the table. At lunchtime, all materials were put back into the crates so we could use the table for lunch. At the end of the school day, the crates (filled with curriculum materials) were placed on a shelf in our mudroom.

A few years ago we finished our basement, so today we are lucky to have a designated room where most of our schooling is done. Each child has a short locker for storing his or her own curriculum materials and supplies. Our schoolroom also has a table, book

5 STEPS TO SUCCESSFUL HOME SCHOOLING

shelves and a storage closet, where we keep everything from our books – textbooks, literature, encyclopedias and references, and home education manuals – to district documents, home school conference brochures, standardized testing information, and craft and project supplies. Having all our home schooling things in one location is of tremendous help, and by working to keep this area clutter free, we can be much more efficient.

The children and I work together to keep our home and schooling materials organized. Often, during the day, we'll do a 'five minute cleanup' time, during which each child is assigned an area of the house to clean (their bedroom, their home school locker, the mudroom, whatever). The timer is set, and I say, "Go!" (You could wave a checkered flag instead if you have one!) Off they race, to get their task completed and return before the timer rings. This is a quick, regular, and effective way to stop clutter from building up!

Whether you do your schooling at the kitchen table or in a study/school area within your home, take time to organize your materials. No one benefits if orange juice spills on math books, toddlers destroy writing assignments left on couches, or registration forms can't be found when it's time to race out for classes. It may not be possible to keep your entire home in complete order during this season of your life. However, do whatever you can to establish and maintain a system of organization for your home school documents and materials.

Step 4: Get Organized!

1. Organize your priorities first!

    a. God

    b. Spouse

    c. Children

    d. Work

2. Discern the number of regular activities and commitments in which you and your children are involved.

3. Schedule your daily routine.

4. Keep home school materials (in the area in which they are used) orderly.

Step 5: Find Support

"I give you a new commandment: love one another. As I have loved you, so you also should love one another." (John 13:34)

We find ourselves at the fifth and final step in successful home schooling. In addition to incorporating regular prayer in our lives, establishing a mission for our home education program, reading quality literature, and organizing our calendars and homes, it is imperative that we find support for our home schooling journey.

People are social beings. We were not created to live in a vacuum or on a deserted island. Although we must strive to be 'not *of* the world', we do live *in* this world. As a home schooling parent, you will face unique challenges and joys. You will have many questions throughout your home education journey, and will want to discuss them with others. Therefore, it's important to know other Christian home schooling parents with whom you can share your thoughts. Likewise, your children will find enormous value in knowing other home schooled youth.

As a home educating adult, you will need many kinds of support. First, you'll want the support of your spouse. Second, find and connect with other Christian home educators in your area. Third,

5 STEPS TO SUCCESSFUL HOME SCHOOLING

realize that legal support is available to home educators. Finally, attend home school conferences as they can be of tremendous value.

THE VALUE OF SPOUSAL SUPPORT

After God, the next most important person to support your home schooling effort is your spouse. If he or she does not agree with your decision to home educate the children, prayerfully consider whether or not this is the best decision for your family. Home schooling is an excellent option, often times the best option, for educating one's children. However, without the support of both spouses, it would be extremely difficult to carry this out successfully. If you truly believe that God is calling you in this direction and your spouse is ambivalent, ask if he or she will consider supporting the effort for one year. Then, continue praying over this decision. The demands of educating your children in addition to regular parenting and running the household can be daunting, and the challenges will be even greater if you do this without the encouragement of your spouse.

Often, at first, one parent will feel strongly about home schooling and the other will go along with it – sometimes reluctantly. Then, after a year or two, when the fruits of the effort are visible, the reluctant spouse becomes a great supporter of home education. Hesitation about doing home education, however, is not the same as outright opposition to it. You and your spouse should discuss this important decision thoroughly, pray over it, and come to an agreement about it.

Once you've obtained your spouse's approval to move forward with home education, be sure he or she is as involved as possible with your home schooling efforts. Most often, one parent will work outside the home to support the family financially while the other carries out the responsibility for teaching. However, it's beneficial to the whole family if both parents are involved in the home education program. There are a number of ways this can happen. First and

86

STEP 5: FIND SUPPORT

foremost, the teaching parent and children should discuss with the other parent what happened during the school day. Second, the teaching parent should involve their spouse in the decision making process related to curriculum options, class and co-op options, and other opportunities. Later, share how each selected program is working. Other ways that non-teaching parents can be involved in home schooling are: joining field trips whenever possible; reading aloud to children at night; helping to correct homework; teaching specific topics, units, or lessons in the evenings or on weekends (for example, lessons in cooking, car maintenance, or physical fitness). Finally, both parents can attend home school conferences.

FIND AND JOIN
A HOME SCHOOL COMMUNITY

As a new home schooling parent, I joined an interdenominational, Christian, home school support group in my area that held monthly meetings for home schooling parents (mostly mothers). For two years, I attended every meeting! Over time, I have gained immeasurable value from the wisdom of the other group members. I've made many new friends, found answers to significant questions, and received an abundance of wonderful new ideas for my home school. We've discussed curriculum options, recommended books, how to balance marriage and home schooling, stages of childhood development, children with special needs, field trip options, drama opportunities, how to handle babies and toddlers while home schooling older children, and how to deal with crisis in the midst of home schooling. My home school group friends are wonderful Christian witnesses who take their faith seriously. I leave every meeting reaffirmed and reenergized.

If you decide to home school, I strongly encourage you to find a local co-op or support group near you. These groups will not only help answer your questions, they will also keep you informed about

5 Steps to Successful Home Schooling

opportunities available to home schoolers in your area. Later in this chapter, you'll find a listing of Catholic and Protestant home schooling groups for each state. To find a support group in your area, contact the group listed for your state. They should be able to direct you to a support group leader in your area.

Remember, personalities and philosophies will vary from group to group, and any one group may or may not match with your own. If you don't feel comfortable with the dynamics of one group after attending a few meetings, find another group or consider forming your own. The latter can be done by talking with the pastor at your church and the pastors of churches near your home to learn of other home schooling families in your parish and area. Even if it takes some effort to connect with other home schooling parents it will be more than worth it.

Consider Participating in Classes, Co-ops, Etc.

Nowadays, opportunities abound in most areas for home schoolers to participate in classes covering a wide range of subjects. These classes can be of great value both to the parent and child. Parents who aren't confident about teaching certain subjects can relieve this anxiety by enrolling their children in classes in those subjects. Often, parents can sit in on the classes, and can thus learn about those subjects while monitoring class activities. Children who participate in classes are typically responsible for assignments with deadlines and tests. Accountability for homework, papers, projects, and presentations can be a good learning experience, especially for children who may not face such tasks at home. Testing – even if it isn't always an accurate way to determine understanding of what's been learned – can help prepare students for higher education where they will often need to take exams (and possibly for certain employment opportunities where exams may be required). In addition, participating in classes gives your children the opportunity to meet other students, work in

STEP 5: FIND SUPPORT

groups, learn from others, and make friends. And, it is one more way to connect with home educating families in your region.

Before enrolling in any on-line courses or local classes, however, be sure to review your mission statement. Carefully consider the needs of your family and the goals you've identified for each of your children. Too many classes could be overwhelming for your children and could add stress to your family's finances and schedule. A careful review of your home school plan will ensure that needs are met and balance is maintained.

KNOW ABOUT AVAILABLE LEGAL SUPPORT

In addition to spousal assistance and the encouragement of local home schooling families, it is sometimes necessary to obtain legal support. Some states and school districts are friendlier to home schoolers than others. States and school districts that are less tolerant may place unnecessary requirements upon home schooling families or even threaten legal action if a student is not enrolled at the local school. In cases like this, legal guidance can be very beneficial. Most states have home school agencies that provide information and guidelines on state and local requirements for home education. To stay abreast of what is required, contact the appropriate organizations and sign up for their newsletters or e-mail updates. In addition, should you need legal assistance, the Home School Legal Defense Association (HSLDA) provides information and counsel. Contact information for state home school groups and the HSLDA are found at the end of this chapter.

89

Attend Home School Conferences

Another way to gain support in your home education journey is by attending home school conferences. Nearly every state in the nation offers annual (or biannual) Catholic, Protestant, and/or secular home education conferences. Excellent speakers come to these events and share their knowledge on many topics related to home education and the Christian family. Vendors also gather at the conferences to display their curricula, offer workshops to explain and demonstrate their materials, and talk with parents individually to answer any questions related to their materials.

Attending home school conferences is an excellent way for home schooling parents to:
- Meet other home schooling families in your state.
- Obtain current information about home education in the state.
- Learn how to teach different subjects.
- See what materials, curriculum options, clubs, classes, activities, and support groups are currently available for your children and family.

Home school conferences provide continuing education for parent educators, as well as tremendous support and encouragement. They are an excellent setting for both parents to re-confirm their decision to home educate, reconnect with other home schooling parents, and plan the next step in their family's home schooling journey.

STEP 5: FIND SUPPORT

HELP YOUR CHILDREN
CONNECT WITH OTHERS

One reason people do not choose home education for their children is the false notion that the children will miss out on beneficial socialization. This idea of socialization is often misunderstood by many. Without question, children who attend public schools spend most of their waking hours (nearly 40 hours per week) with other children their age who have a tremendous influence on their behavior. When pondering your children's socialization, ask yourself: Who do I most want to influence my children and their behavior – we, their parents, or other children? Do I really want another nine year old to teach my son how to speak to adults? Can an eighth grade girl teach my daughter what she needs to know about true friendship and how to treat others? Do I want other teenagers to teach my son how to behave toward women? If you answered yes to any of these questions, then home schooling may not be your best choice. However, if *you* would like to shape your children's character; if *you* would like to instruct your children on moral conduct; if *you* would like to teach your children how to interact properly with people older or younger than they are, then home education is a wonderful option.

A quick look into a class at your local public high school will confirm that socialization is going on. However, is the teen behavior that you see admirable? Is it what you want your children to emulate? Home schooling offers a different type of socialization, one that conforms more closely to your moral beliefs and code of conduct. Furthermore, it provides opportunity for regular interaction with other children and adults of all ages – a model of interaction that more closely resembles the 'real world'. Few people go to jobs every day where they work only with people of their same age. Families, neighborhoods, churches, and communities are comprised of people of all age groups.

91

5 STEPS TO SUCCESSFUL HOME SCHOOLING

Realize that during your home education journey, it is important for your children to have home schooling friends in your area, whether they meet them through classes, drama clubs, book clubs, Little Flowers or Blue Knights (Catholic girls' and boys' groups similar to Girl and Boy Scouts), athletic clubs, or through local co-ops. Having friends who are also home educated will help your children see that they are not the only home schooling family in the world, and give them companions to spend time with on field trips or activities just for fun. Having these friendships can help your child to not feel lonely if they are the only ones on the local sports team or in the church youth choir who doesn't attend the district school.

One way to find and meet home educated children near you is by contacting your local home school agency. Ask about home school classes, co-ops, and children's groups in your area. If there are none, consider creating your own class (knitting, table tennis, foreign language, literature, etc.) or club (drama, ski, book, etc.) or hosting an event (game night, snow tubing, etc.) and invite other home school students in your area to join you. The local home school agency can help you spread the word about your event. The value you will receive for your effort is sure to be high.

Another simple way to become acquainted with other home educated children in your area is to attend a home school Mass at a parish near you. If you can't find one, consider helping to get one started at your own church or another parish nearby. As mentioned previously, our family attends Mass every Friday morning with other home school families from our area. The children proclaim the readings, provide music, and serve as acolytes. There is fellowship after each Mass. In other areas, home schooling families gather for First Friday Masses or children's adoration hour followed by fellowship. Finally, your pastor may be able to help you connect with home schooling families from your parish or neighboring parishes.

STEP 5: FIND SUPPORT

OBTAIN NECESSARY RESOURCES
TO EDUCATE CHILDREN WITH SPECIAL NEEDS

Many home schooling families find blessings and support in home educating their special needs children. If your child has special needs, realize that you are not alone. According to John Tuma, Minnesota Association of Christian Home Educators (MÂCHÉ) board member and attorney, "Providing an education for the special needs child will have its challenges regardless of the educational approach taken. Homeschooling provides a wonderful educational opportunity for special needs children and their families, and I would go as far as to say that it is the best educational option for the special needs child" (Tuma 1).

Today, there are more resources than ever available for children with extraordinary needs. However, finding the most appropriate resources for your particular situation may be difficult. Be aware, also, that some school districts may challenge your right to educate special needs children at home. Therefore, it is important to obtain the legal information and support you need. The Home School Legal Defense Association (HSLDA) is an excellent organization to contact, if you are currently home schooling a child with special needs (or intend to do so). In addition to legal support, this organization provides the expert advice of a special needs coordinator who can direct you to resources suitable for your child and his or her situation. These resources include recommended articles, books, curricula, testing services, professional services in your area, supplies, sports and recreation information, evaluation tests and services, and other materials related to the specific needs of your child. I have found their services to be quite helpful. An excellent starting point for any parent considering home education as an option for their special needs child is an article printed in the HSLDA publication *The Home School Court Report* titled, "Growing at Home: Nourishing Your

93

5 STEPS TO SUCCESSFUL HOME SCHOOLING

Special Needs Child" (May/June 2005).

Contact information for the Home School Legal Defense Association is listed on the following pages.

The support of other home educating families in your area will help you and your children (with or without special needs) meet the unique challenges you're sure to face as home schoolers. Take advantage of the support available in your area, which can be found by contacting one of the organizations listed on the following pages.

National Home School Organizations and Resources for Catholic Home Educators:

The following pages list Catholic and Protestant home school agencies and groups by state. Use this list as a starting point to get connected with others in your area. Most groups are run by parent volunteers and list an Internet address as their means for contact. At the time of this printing, the information below was current. However, some may have disbanded or changed their contact information by the time you read this. A quick search on the Internet will help you find current information in your area.

Home School Legal Defense Association
P.O. Box 3000
Purcellville, VA 20134-9000
540-338-5600
www.hslda.org

National Challenged Homeschoolers Association Network (NATHAN)
P.O. Box 310
Moyie Springs, ID 83845
www.NATHAN.com

National Association of Catholic Home Educators
P.O. Box 4
Clayton, DE 19938
703-553-9600
www.nache.org

5 STEPS TO SUCCESSFUL HOME SCHOOLING

Catholic Homeschool Support (on-line support site)
www.catholichomeschool.org

United States Conference of Catholic Bishops website (excellent Catholic resources including daily mass readings)
usccb.org

Relevant Radio-Catholic radio station
www.relevantradio.com
(website lists local stations – or listen on-line)

Alabama
Catholic Home Educators of Mobile
jenjenwh@catholicexchange.com

Immaculate Heart of Mary Homeschool Group
rjmack@ardmore.net

Christian Home Education Fellowship of Alabama
www.chefofalabama.org
334-288-7229

Alaska
Alaska Private and Home Educator's Association
P.O. Box 14174
Anchorage, AK 99514
www.aphea.org

Arizona
Holy Family Home Educators
hfhe@mac.com

Sacred Hearts Home Educators
webmaster@shhe.net

Step 5: Find Support

Arizona Families for Home Education
www.afhe.org
800-929-3927

Arkansas
Greater Fort Smith Catholic Homeschoolers
greaterfortsmithcatholichomeschoolers@yahoogroups.com

St. Gabriel Catholic Homeschool Group
melanievogel@yahoo.com

Home Educators of Arkansas
www.geocities.com/heartland/garden/4555/hear.html

California
California Homeschool Network
www.californiahomeschool.net
800-327-5339

Southern California Catholic Home Educators
www.scchehomepage.com
scche@earthlink.net

Colorado
Rocky Mountain Catholic Home Educators Conference
www.rmchec.org
303-750-9522

Christian Home Educators of Colorado
www.chec.org
720-842-4852

Connecticut
Catholic Home Educators in Connecticut
Cath_Home_Ed_in_CT@hotmail.com

5 STEPS TO SUCCESSFUL HOME SCHOOLING

The Education Association of Christian Homeschoolers of
Connecticut
www.teachct.org
860-793-9968

Delaware
St. Ambrose
saintambrose@yahoogroups.com

St. John Bosco Catholic Homeschoolers of Delaware
rchiasson@comcast.ent

Delaware Home Education Association
www.dheaonline.org

Florida
Florida Network of Catholic Home Educators
fnche@aol.com

Immaculate Heart of Mary Home School and Parent Conferences
ihmconference.org/tampa

Christian Home Educators of Florida
www.christianhomeeducatorsofflorida.com

Georgia
ARCH of Georgia (Association of Roman Catholic Homeschoolers)
Archofgeorgia-owner@yahoogroups.com

Catholic Homeschool Conference
www.chsconferencega.com

Georgia Home Education Association
www.ghea.org
770-461-3657

98

STEP 5: FIND SUPPORT

Hawaii
Our Lady of Fatima Catholic Homeschoolers of Hawaii
esther@catholicweb.com

TORCH: Catholic Homeschooler of Hawaii
www.catholichome.homestead.com

Christian Home Educators of Maui
www.hispraise.com/chem

Idaho
Catholic Home Educators of Treasure Valley
CHEofTV-owner@yahoogroups.com

Christian Homeschoolers of Idaho State
www.chois.org
208-424-6685

Illinois
Network of Illinois Catholic Home Educators (NICHE)
www.nichejmj.com
708-428-4540

Illinois Christian Home Educators
www.iche.org
815-943-7882

Indiana
Holy Family Home Educators
www.hfheindy.org
317-786-3629

Indiana Association of Home Educators
www.inhomeeducators.org
317-859-1202

99

5 STEPS TO SUCCESSFUL HOME SCHOOLING

Iowa
Columbus Academy: Supporting Catholic Home-Educating Families
in Iowa
www.homeschool-life.com

Network of Iowa Christian Home Educators
www.the-niche.org
800-723-0438

Kansas
Holy Family Home Educators of Wichita
www.hfhewichita.org

Kansas City Conference for Catholic Homeschoolers
www.kccatholichomeschool.org
816-454-3729

Christian Home Educators Confederation of Kansas
www.kansashomeschool.org
785-272-6655

Kentucky
St. Benedict Homeschool Association
www.kycatholichomeschooling.org
270-307-6777
270-307-6326

Christian Home Educators of Kentucky
www.chek.org
270-358-9270

Louisiana
Roman Catholic Homeschool Association of Louisiana
www.rchal.org
985-809-0899

STEP 5: FIND SUPPORT

Christian Home Educators Fellowship of Louisiana
www.chefofla.org

Maine
Catholic Homeschooling Moms
sixarewe@yahoo.com

Homeschoolers of Maine
www.homeschoolersofmaine.org/index.htm

Maryland
Maryland Roman Catholic Homeschool
Mrch-owner@yahoogroups.com

Mother Seton TORCH of Montgomery County
www.montgomerytorch.org

Maryland Association of Christian Home Educators
www.machemd.org
301-607-4284

Massachusetts
Boston Catholic Homeschoolers
Bostoncatholics-owner@yahoogroups.com

Massachusetts Homeschool Organization of Parent Educators
www.masshope.org

Michigan
Michigan Catholic Home Educators
www.rc.net/lansing/mch

Information Network for Christian Homes
www.inch.org
616-874-5656

101

Minnesota
MN Catholic Home Education Conference
www.mnconference.org
info@mnconference.org

Minnesota Association of Christian Home Educators
www.mache.org
763-717-9070

Mississippi
Mississippi Catholic Home Educators
jmurphymom@juno.com
601-829-4468

Mississippi Home Educator's Association
www.mhea.net
662-578-6432

Missouri
St. Louis Catholic Homeschool Association
www.stlouiscatholichomeschool.com

Missouri Association of Teaching Christian Homes
www.match-inc.org
815-550-8641

Montana
Montana Coalition of Home Educators
www.mtche.org

Nebraska
Omaha Catholic Homeschool Conference
www.chaoconference.com
402-490-9792

STEP 5: FIND SUPPORT

Nebraska Christian Home Educators Association
402-423-4297
www.nchea.org

Nevada
Catholic Homeschoolers of Nevada: Our Lady of Perpetual Help
Home Educators
dinareenall@yahoo.com

Nevada Homeschool Network
www.nevadahomeschoolnetwork.com

New Hampshire
CHURCH: Catholic Homeschoolers Uniting Religion, Community,
and Home
catholicschoolers@yahoo.com
207-339-8897

Pilgrims of the Holy Family
phfemail@catholicexchange.com

Christian Home Educators of New Hampshire
www.mv.com/ipusers/chenh

New Jersey
CHAPLET: Catholic Homeschool Association with Papal Loyalty
Educating Together
www.chaplet.org

Education Network of Christian Home Schoolers of New Jersey
www.enochnj.org

New Mexico
Corpus Christi Home Educators
Cchenm.org

103

5 STEPS TO SUCCESSFUL HOME SCHOOLING

Holy Faith Home Educators
Holyfaithmed.homestead.com
HolyFaithHmEd@aol.com

Christian Association of Parent Educators of New Mexico
505-898-8548

New York
Buffalo Catholic Homeschooling Conference
www.quietwatersproductions.com

Children of Mary Homeschoolers
www.childrenofmaryhomeschoolers.org

Actively and Positively Parenting and Lovingly Educating
www.APPLEnetwork.US/ny/apple.html

North Carolina
ARCH of the Triangle: Association of Roman Catholic
Homeschoolers
http://arch-raleigh.ning.com
919-649-7667

North Carolinians for Home Education
www.nche.com
919-790-1100

North Dakota
FACHE: Fargo Area Catholic Home Educators
rmsayler@juno.com

SW ND Catholic Homeschoolers
little@ndsupernet.com

104

STEP 5: FIND SUPPORT

North Dakota Home School Association
www.ndhsa.org
701-223-4080

Ohio
The Immaculate Heart of Mary Homeschool and Parent Conferences
www.ihmconference.org/cleveland
540-636-1946

Christian Home Educators of Ohio
www.cheohome.org

Oklahoma
St. Gianna Homeschool Group
stgianna@yahoogroups.com
nowensl@cox.net

Christian Home Educators Fellowship of Oklahoma
www.chefok.org
918-583-7323

Oregon
Catholic Lane
CatholicLane@yahoogroups.com

Holy Family Home Educators
crjantzer@msn.com

Oregon Christian Hme Education Association Network
www.oceanetwork.org/lowres.cfm
503-288-1285

Pennsylvania
Catholic Homeschoolers of Pennsylvania
www.catholichomeschoolpa.org
717-866-5425

5 STEPS TO SUCCESSFUL HOME SCHOOLING

Christian Homeschool Association of Pennsylvania
www.chapboard.org/Home.html

Rhode Island
Rhode Island Guild of Home Teachers
www.rihomeschool.com

South Carolina
Carolina Catholic HSers
www.egroups.com/group/CarolinaCatholicHS

South Carolina Association of Independent Home Schools
www.scaihs.org

South Dakota
St. Margaret's Fellowship
Stmargaret.homestead.com

South Dakota Christian Home Educators
www.sdche.org/sdche.html
605-348-2001

Tennessee
Blessed Sacrament Homeschool Group
5955 St. Elmo
Bartlett, TN 38134
901-382-2504

Tennessee Home Education Association
www.tnhea.org
858-623-7899

Texas
Immaculate Heart of Mary Conference
www.ihmconference.org/northtexas

STEP 5: FIND SUPPORT

ARCH: Apostolate of Roman Catholic Homeschoolers
www.arch-homeschool.org
281-797-5578

Christian Home Educators Association of Central Texas
www.cheact.org
512-450-0070

Utah
Utah Homeschool Support
Utahcatholichomeschoolers-owner@yahoogroups.com

Utah Christian Home School Association
www.utch.org
801-296-7198

Vermont
Vermont Roman Catholic Homeschooling Group
larossi@together.net

Vermont Association of Home Educators
www.vermonthomeschool.org

Virginia
Immaculate Heart of Mary National Conference
www.ihmconference.org/national
IHM Coalition
P.O. Box 574
Linden, VA 22642
540-636-1946

Virginia Home Education Association
www.vhea.org

5 STEPS TO SUCCESSFUL HOME SCHOOLING

Washington

Catholic Homeschoolers of Olympia
catholichomeschoolersofolympia@yahoogroups.com

Northwest Catholic Family Education Conference
www.nwcatholicconference.com
206-230-0455

St. Joseph Catholic Homeschool
Saintjosephhomeschool.blogspot.com

Washington Association of Teaching Christian Homes
www.watchhome.org
206-729-4804

West Virginia

St. James TORCH
infor@torchwv.org

Christian Home Educators of West Virginia
www.chewv.org

Wisconsin

Greater Milwaukee Catholic Home Educators
www.gmche.com
gmchegroup@gmail.com

Sacred Heart Home Schoolers
www.homeschool-life.com/wi/shh
ta2ems@hotmail.com

Twin Ports L.O.V.E. (Our Lady of Victory Educators)
stephw@gnsconsulting.com

STEP 5: FIND SUPPORT

Wisconsin Christian Home Educators Association
www.wisconsinchea.com
262-637-5127

Wyoming
Catholic H.E.A.R.T. of Wyoming
Wychs-subscribe@yahoogroups.com

Homeschoolers of Wyoming
www.homeschoolersofwy.org

Step 5: Find Support

1. The support of your spouse is very important.

2. Consider joining a local home school support group or participating in or creating home school clubs, classes, or activities with your children.

3. Know where to find legal support if needed.

4. Attend home school conferences whenever possible.

5. Ensure that your kids connect with other home schooled children.

6. Take advantage of available resources for home schooling children with special needs.

BONUS SECTION

How to Begin Home Schooling Quickly

As mentioned at the beginning of this book, a few years ago, a friend asked me how to begin home schooling her son. She would have loved to have had the opportunity to attend conferences, research curriculum materials for a year, and talk with other home schooling families. Unfortunately, she did not have the luxury of time. She needed to begin home schooling her son almost immediately.

My friend's quick decision to home school her son came about due to a tragedy he experienced at school. Although athletic, intelligent, handsome, and friendly, this young man became the target of bullying when he switched to a new school.

One would like to think that bullying does not exist in Christian schools, but unfortunately, it does. And, although parents, teachers, and administrators may step in and try to resolve the issues, positive outcomes are not always the result. This was the case with my friend's child. Due to the severity of the on-going bullying, he left this new school at the end of the first semester and did not return.

The impact that this negative experience had on my friend's son is difficult to express in words. The fear, rejection, humiliation, and

111

confusion that came from the subjection to daily physical and emotional abuse caused deep wounds that took much time to heal. Wisely, his parents recognized this and put every effort into helping their son recover from his emotional wounds. I can only imagine the comfort and security he must have felt to be safe at home in the loving care of his parents. Finally, day by day, week by week, he regained his sense of security and value, largely due to his parents' loving care. I am happy to say that this young man is thriving today.

Some of you may have experienced similar situations. For you, home schooling is not a decision made after careful prayer, rigorous study about different education options, and much discussion with other home school families. For some, as for my friend, it is a necessity that's come about due to negative experiences taking place at your child's school. Some kids are bullied on the playground or the school bus, while others struggle with abusive teachers or staff members. Removing a child from these types of situations may be required for the child's safety or mental health, and home schooling may be a necessity.

Other reasons for looking at home education for children without much time to plan include family transitions, such as, a new job for someone in the family, a job loss, a move, a family health crisis, extended travel, a birth, a death, a divorce, a decision to go out on the mission field, an athletic opportunity, etc. Ideally, it's preferred to have a year to prepare to home school, but that's not how it always works out. If you must make a quick start to home schooling, these steps will guide you. Realize that you are not alone and that a quick start does not mean that your chances for success are any less than someone who spent years preparing. Be confident in knowing that you and your children can find tremendous blessing and success through home education.

BONUS SECTION

FIVE STEPS TO A QUICK START

Step 1: Pause and Pray

Our former pastor used to quote his father once in a while. His dad, who instilled the value of hard work, perseverance, and prayer in his twelve children, said, "When you're in a hurry, take your time." How true this is. It seems that most mistakes come about when we are trying to rush. This holds true for home schooling. Before diving into the work, slow down, pause, catch your breath, and pray.

It is natural to be anxious when beginning to home school – especially if you're starting the process hastily; possibly mid-year, mid-semester, or even mid-week. Considering the amount of home work kids come home with nowadays, and the current obsession with testing and grades, you'll probably feel an urgency to hurry up and get your kids working on something so they don't fall behind. Do not believe this fallacy. Take the time you need to pause and pray. Your child will not be harmed if you take a week, a month, even a semester to fully begin. In fact, they will likely be blessed by taking time to heal and find peace through the adjustment process.

If you are removing your child from a negative school experience, allow him or her the time needed to heal, without piling on science homework or grammar practice that could worsen his or her morale. In this case, simply letting your children relax and play, reading with them, working on math worksheets, and going on field trips together will provide enough education while you adjust to the new schooling situation.

Although the decision to home educate may have come about quickly, it is not necessary to rush heedlessly into busy work. Take time to

113

5 STEPS TO SUCCESSFUL HOME SCHOOLING

pray alone, with your spouse, and with your child. Ask God for guidance, wisdom, and peace in your decision to home school.

Step 2: Establish your immediate mission

As discussed earlier in the book, it is important to understand the direction in which you are heading before you begin the journey. It is also important to ask the right questions before getting started. If you find yourself beginning to home school on short notice, consider asking the following questions and looking into the appropriate actions.

1. What are the emotional needs of my child? Is counseling necessary?
2. What are the current social, academic, and spiritual needs of my child?
3. How do I plan to address the above listed needs?
4. How much time can I give my child to help them adjust to their current situation? What are the best steps for me to take to help with this adjustment?
5. What are the educational requirements of my state?
   a. Contact a local home school agency to answer this question. Some school districts are hostile toward home schooling and will be reluctant to give you the required documentation needed, and they may try to discourage you from home educating your child. The "Find Support" Section of this book lists many home school groups and agencies that can provide you with the required documentation and information.
   b. Which subjects are necessary to begin immediately? Can I delay the start of certain subjects to allow my child more time to adjust to the new routine and heal from any emotional wounds?
6. What adjustments do I need to make to my current commitments? (Consider how you will adjust work schedules, volunteer commitments, social activities, etc.)
7. What type of home school program will work best for my

114

child, for me as the home educator, and for our family?

    a. The appendix lists different curriculum options and programs. Some programs are as easy as ordering '6th Grade in a Box'. These comprehensive programs will provide you with all of the materials needed for a selected grade, along with teacher support. Other programs allow you to customize the curriculum based upon the needs of your child. If your child was in the middle of studying American history, for example, it might be natural to choose an American history text to continue this study, rather than switching to ancient history, European history, or some other social studies program. See the appendix for programs and curriculum ordering information.

8. Will my child benefit from participating in a class, a club, or another program with other home schooled youth? Or, is it best to limit the amount of running around we do and spend more time focused on emotional support at home? What balance is best for my child?

9. What kind of support do I (the parent) need?

    a. Chapter five of this book discusses different home school support groups and options. Many are easy to find on-line. In addition, depending upon the situation with your child, counseling may be necessary for you. If so, carefully choose the therapist with whom you choose to work. Not all therapists are supportive of Christianity, nor are all therapists supportive of home schooling. Find a counselor that respects your beliefs and with whom you feel comfortable. It may take some 'shopping around' before you find a therapist with whom you feel comfortable working.

Take time to answer these questions before rushing headlong into an

5 STEPS TO SUCCESSFUL HOME SCHOOLING

unplanned agenda. Being careful and intentional about your education program will be of greater value than racing into something that has not been well thought out. If it takes a week or two (or even longer) to figure out your program and obtain your materials, do not fear. Education and healing can begin.

Step 3: Read!

There is a lot of truth to the old standard of the three R's (reading, writing, and arithmetic). While taking time to figure out the best plan of action for your unique situation and while waiting for curriculum materials to arrive; you can take great educational steps. First and foremost, read! Chapter 3 of this book provides book lists for each grade level that you can use as a starting point. Go to the library and check out a number of the recommended books. Then, schedule time each day for your child to read one book independently and one book with you. As mentioned earlier, reading aloud to your children provides immeasurable benefits, not the least of which is a sense of security, love, and routine, as you snuggle on the couch and read together. Discussing what happens in these books may even be therapeutic as you consider the experiences (similar to your own or vastly different) of the book characters. Reading great literature is one of the best forms of education you can offer your child, and it can be done immediately and (thanks to the library) at minimal or no cost.

A very simple program for home education - a way to begin before fully preparing an educational plan, is to:
1. Spend one hour each day reading aloud to your children.
2. Have the child spend one hour each day reading on their own. For younger children who are unable to read, allow them to look at picture books for 30 minutes and listen to a book on tape for thirty minutes. Older children who have difficulty reading on their own can simply listen to an audio book for the full hour.
3. Spend 30-60 minutes a day working with math. If you have not yet ordered a math curriculum (see appendix for

116

recommendations), many excellent math worksheets are available on-line. In addition, there are many wonderful games that use math (cribbage, Allowance, Monopoly, etc.). And, of course, math can be used during real life activities such as a trip to the grocery store or while baking at home (great fractions practice).

4. Encourage writing. Allot 30 minutes each day for your kids to work on a weekly writing assignment. For example: Week 1: have the children research something of interest to them and write a report on that topic; Week 2: invite them to write a poem; Week 3: have your child write letters to friends and/or relatives; Week 4: help them create short stories. Repeat this sequence, giving topics of focus for their research, poetry, and stories. For example, have them research a famous scientist and write a report on that person. Then they could compose poems about the scientist or an area of study on which the scientist focused. Next, they could create a short story based upon the life of that person. (You could do the same for a famous historical character.)

5. Consider possible field trips. Trips to local museums, parks, libraries, music halls, theatres, and businesses of interest (i.e. newspapers, radio stations, etc.) can all provide excellent and interesting educational experiences. In addition, consider taking a field trip outside of your locale. Home schooling allows for travel at 'low peak' times throughout the year. Our family went to the Grand Canyon in May, before the regular tourist crowds descended during the summer months. We had great weather, wonderful accommodations, discounted rates, and an excellent time – without the frustration of crowds.

Following these five steps will provide your children a rich education while you figure out the specifics of the rest of the home school program. Do not underestimate the value of reading and researching. Combining these activities with some math practice, writing oppor-

5 STEPS TO SUCCESSFUL HOME SCHOOLING

tunities, and interesting field trips will go a long way in your child's educational development.

Step 4: Get Organized

It may seem impossible to get organized when life feels as though it's been turned upside down. However, it is possible and important to structure your days.

As mentioned earlier in Step Four, planning the home school day can be boiled down to these two rules of thumb: identify your priorities and establish a routine. If you are beginning quickly, review the questions listed in Step #2 of this section. Answering these questions will help you to recognize your immediate priorities. Identify the needs of your children (for example, counseling or therapy sessions, time to get to know other home schooled youth, etc.) to ensure that you schedule activities to meet those needs first when you create a schedule. Once these items have been identified and scheduled, come up with a routine to be followed each week. It will be comforting for the child to know what to expect from each day. Even if you have not figured out your entire home education program, an interim schedule will be comforting as it will help you all know what to expect each day.

When making a daily schedule, identify a time to begin your work each day. Allowing the children to sleep in all morning and awaken whenever they desire is neither healthy nor practical. On the other hand, if your child requires more sleep or is not an early riser, it is unwise to begin your day at 5:00am. Establish a start time, and stick with this. Then, outline the routine for each day. For example:

Monday
8:00am	Wake up. Make bed. Get dressed. Breakfast.
9:00am	Begin day with prayer. Complete math worksheets.
10:00am	Listen to mom read aloud a book.
11:00am	Take a walk or other form of physical activity.

11:30am	Research project.
Noon	Lunch.
1:00pm	Read or listen to book on tape for one hour.
2:00pm	Practice musical instrument or complete household chores.

One last note regarding the schedule: people often say to my children how nice it must be to be able to do school work in their pajamas. We smile at this comment, but do not reply. Only one day each school year are my children allowed to do their school work in their pajamas. They look forward to it each year, as we call it 'Pajama Day' and often do some fun games and activities, and eat breakfast food for lunch. It is important for children, no matter what their situation, to get up, washed, and dressed at the start of each day. We all feel better and perform better when we are clean and dressed. Remaining in pajamas all day could lead to sluggishness and laziness. Although you may be slowly easing into your home education plan, don't let your children to think they are on a vacation for six months. Even if you spend your days reading on the couch and taking a walk in the park, unless a child is ill, it's important that kids brush their teeth, comb their hair, and get dressed.

Step 5: Find Support

If you must begin home schooling with little upfront preparation, please read Step 5 in this book right away. That chapter contains a great deal of information about support networks available for parents and children in the world of home education, including support for those who are home schooling special needs children.

If you are leaving a negative school situation, if you have recently moved to a new city or state, or if you are experiencing a family crisis and have recently decided to home school, look into support options for your children. It may be wise to contact a Catholic or Christian home school group in your area and ask for recommendations. It may also be helpful to talk with your parish priest or your pediatrician.

5 STEPS TO SUCCESSFUL HOME SCHOOLING

The suggestions in this book are presented as recommendations and do not take the place of the wisdom of someone who knows you and your situation personally.

Finally, contact a local home school group or your state department of education to determine what documentation is required for home schoolers. Each state has unique requirements. Although these forms may not need to be turned in right away, eventually they will have to be done.

Do not feel that you need to make this journey alone. There are many resources available and many people willing to offer their help and guidance. If you are having a difficult time knowing where to begin when looking for support, I encourage you to contact the Home School Legal Defense Association. This national organization provides a wealth of resources and has connections throughout the nation. Their contact information is:

Home School Legal Defense Association
P.O. Box 3000
Purcellville, VA 20134-9000
540-338-5600
www.hslda.org

Jumping into home schooling with little or no preparation can seem overwhelming. However, it can be done, and done very successfully. Put these five steps into practice and you will be off to an excellent start with your children.

BONUS SECTION

GETTING STARTED QUICKLY

1. Pray!

2. Identify the immediate needs of your child. Determine ways to meet those needs.

3. Read! Establish a daily routine that includes reading, writing, and math practice. Begin to research curriculum options for your child. (See Appendix B)

4. Organize your daily schedule. Begin at a set time each day. Follow a daily routine.

5. Find support for you and your child. Complete required state documentation for home schooling. Contact local home school group, national home school agency, parish priest, or pediatrician.

Conclusion

"The right and duty of parents to give education is essential since it is connected with the transmission of human life; it is original and primary with regard to the educational role of others, on account of the uniqueness of the living relationship between parents and children; and it is irreplaceable and inalienable, and therefore incapable of being entirely delegated to others or usurped by others."
Blessed Pope John Paul II

There is a riddle some home schoolers like to tell. It goes like this: What do Benjamin Franklin, C.S. Lewis, Thomas Jefferson, and Abraham Lincoln all have in common? The answer: They were all home schooled. Most people would look at these individuals and agree that they attained success in their lives. Clearly, their home education experience did not limit their abilities. Indeed, it is likely that their home schooling actually encouraged and fostered their gifts. And, they achieved this success without the benefit of home school co-ops, conferences, or curriculum materials!

If you are considering home education for your children, I encourage you to give it a try. It is a big decision, and you may have some fear about taking the next step. It is my hope that this book will give you the courage and the tools necessary to take that step, and to take it with confidence.

For those of you who have been home educating your children

already, my wish for you is that this book will give you ideas and inspiration to continue on this transforming journey.

Without question, it is possible to achieve success through home education. Fortunately, there is no mystery to realizing this goal. It is not something that only those who have earned doctorates in education or mothers of days-gone-by can understand. No, the steps to achieving success in home schooling are very clear: through regular prayer, establishing a mission, reading great literature, becoming organized, and finding support, all can realize the goals they have prayerfully prepared for their children.

Appendix A

How to Pray the Rosary

1. Begin at the crucifix which hangs by five beads. Hold on to the crucifix and make the sign of the cross and pray the Apostles' Creed.

2. Next, move your hand to the first bead and recite the Our Father.

3. Move to the next bead and pray a Hail Mary. Then, move to the following bead and pray a second Hail Mary. Repeat this one more time while moving to the next bead.

4. Finally, with fingers on the chain between the fourth bead and the fifth bead, pray the Glory Be.

5. Move fingers to the fifth bead. Announce the first mystery and pray the Our Father.

6. Move fingers to the first group of ten beads. Hold the first bead and pray the Hail Mary. Repeat the Hail Mary nine additional times (for a total of ten Hail Marys) while reflecting upon the first mystery.

5 STEPS TO SUCCESSFUL HOME SCHOOLING

7. Upon completing the tenth Hail Mary, place fingers upon the chain between the last bead in that group and the large bead which begins the next mystery. Recite the Glory Be. (Optional: recite the Fatima Prayer following the Glory Be) This completes the first mystery of the rosary (often referred to as the first decade of the rosary).

8. Begin the next mystery by holding on to the large bead found next on the rosary. Announce the second mystery and pray the Our Father.

9. Repeat steps 5 through 7 until all five mysteries have been prayed.

10. Following the recitation of the Our Father, ten Hail Marys, Glory Be and Fatima prayer for each mystery, hold on to the center medal (often an image of Mary is engraved upon this center piece). Pray the Hail Holy Queen.

PRAYERS OF THE ROSARY

THE SIGN OF THE CROSS
In the name of the Father, and of the Son, and of the Holy Spirit. Amen.

THE APOSTLES' CREED
I believe in God, the Father Almighty, Creator of heaven and earth; and in Jesus Christ, His only Son, our Lord; Who was conceived by the Holy Spirit, born of the Virgin Mary, suffered under Pontius Pilate, was crucified, died, and was buried. He descended into hell; the third day He arose again from the dead. He ascended into Heaven, and sits at the right hand of God, the Father Almighty; from thence He shall come to judge the living and the dead. I believe in the Holy Spirit, the Holy Catholic Church, the communion of Saints, the forgiveness of sins, the resurrection of the body, and life everlasting. Amen.

APPENDIX A

THE OUR FATHER
Our Father, Who art in Heaven, hallowed be Thy name; Thy Kingdom come, Thy will be done on earth as it is in Heaven. Give us this day our daily bread; and forgive us our trespasses as we forgive those who trespass against us, and lead us not into temptation, but deliver us from evil. Amen.

HAIL MARY
Hail Mary, full of Grace, the Lord is with thee. Blessed art thou among women, and blessed is the fruit of thy womb, Jesus. Holy Mary, Mother of God, pray for us sinners, now and at the hour of our death. Amen.

THE DOXOLOGY (The Glory Be)
Glory be to the Father, and to the Son, and to the Holy Spirit. As it was in the beginning, is now, and ever shall be, world without end. Amen.

FATIMA PRAYER
O my Jesus, forgive us our sins, save us from the fires of hell, lead all souls to Heaven, especially those in most need of Thy mercy. Amen.

HAIL, HOLY QUEEN (Salve Regina)
Hail Holy Queen, Mother of Mercy, our life, our sweetness and our hope! To thee do we cry, poor banished children of Eve; to thee do we send up our sighs, mourning and weeping in this valley of tears. Turn then, most gracious advocate, Thine eyes of mercy toward us, and after this our exile, show unto us the blessed fruit of Thy womb, Jesus. O clement, O loving, O sweet Virgin Mary!

> V. Pray for us, O Holy Mother of God.
> R. That we may be made worthy of the promises of Christ.

Let us pray. O God, whose only begotten Son, by His life, death, and resurrection, has purchased for us the rewards of eternal life, grant, we beseech Thee, that meditating upon these mysteries of the Most Holy Rosary of the Blessed Virgin Mary, we may imitate what they contain and obtain what they promise, through the same Christ Our

127

Lord. Amen.

Recommendation:
An excellent resource for children to learn the rosary is a small book by Fr. Lovasik, S.V.D. titled *The Holy Rosary*. This thirty-two page book provides an easy to read history of the rosary, a step-by-step guide for praying the rosary, as well as additional prayers to Our Lady and beautiful pictures. It is published by Catholic Book Publishing Co. New York.

APPENDIX B

CURRICULUM PROVIDERS
AND OTHER RESOURCES

Most of the providers listed below are Catholic curriculum providers. However, some of the curriculum providers listed are neither Catholic nor Protestant. As with any book or subject matter, it is the parent's responsibility to review all books and resources before sharing them with their children. Non-Catholic resources may contain material that is not in keeping with the teachings of the Church. For a math program, for example, where neither Church history nor Church doctrine is discussed, this may not pose a problem. However, for a history text or a piece of literature, caution should be observed when offering these materials to your children. Some of these non-Catholic resources may contain material that is hostile toward or in contradiction with the Catholic Church. As of this printing, I recommend the programs listed below and have used materials from them. However, programs, books, and websites can change. Likewise, what was appropriate for my children may not be appropriate for yours. Please use discretion when selecting your resources.

ANGELICUM ACADEMY HOMESCHOOL PROGRAM
Mission statement: The Angelicum Academy Homeschool Program

5 STEPS TO SUCCESSFUL HOME SCHOOLING

is a nursery-12th grade curriculum for home education. It is complete – including all subjects, books, guides and tests needed, for all grades. Optional services for enrolled students include grading, transcript maintenance, online literature discussion classes and the finest online resources (such as Encyclopaedia Britannica and the Merriam-Webster Dictionary). Our Great Books Program may be taken for high school, college credit, or both. The Angelicum Academy, founded in 2000 A.D., is officially recognized by the Church as a Catholic home school program.

Contact information:
Angelicum Academy Homeschool and Great Books Program
Phone: 816-220-2626
Fax: 816-220-2727
E-mail: AngelicumMailbox@aol.com

Mailing Address
Angelicum Academy
PO Box 47
Manitou Springs, CO 80829

Web address: www.angelicum.net

CATHOLIC HOME SCHOOLING: A Handbook for Parents
Excellent resource discussing many topics related to home schooling. Written by Mary Kay Clark and published by Seton Home Study School Press.

Web address: www.setonhome.org

DESIGNING YOUR OWN CLASSICAL CURRICULUM: A Guide to Catholic Home Education.
This book is an excellent resource for all Catholic home educators. It offers suggested course work, subject resources, and reading lists for every grade in a child's education. It is a book I refer to often. A must have resource for all Catholic home educators. Published

130

APPENDIX B

by Ignatius Press. Sold by most Catholic home school resource providers.

Web address: www.emmanuelbooks.com

EMMANUEL BOOKS
A family business serving the needs of families. Specializing in Catholic educational material, particularly Classic Curricula. Official "Mother of Divine Grace" curriculum provider.

Contact information:
Phone: 800-871-5598
(International callers use: 302-325-9515)
FAX #: 302-325-4336

Mailing Address
P. O. Box 321
New Castle, DE 19720
Email: email@emmanuelbooks.com
Web address: www.emmanuelbooks.com

KOLBE ACADEMY
Kolbe Academy's focus is on providing a Catholic education that is Ignatian in Method, Classical in Content and Loyal to the Magisterium in a small-class size environment or at home.

Contact information:
Phone: 707-255-6499
Fax: 707-255-1581

Mailing address:
Kolbe Academy
1600 F Street
Napa, CA 94559

Web address: www.kolbe.org

5 STEPS TO SUCCESSFUL HOME SCHOOLING

MOTHER OF DIVINE GRACE

Mission statement: A Catholic distance education program dedicated to helping homeschoolers design their own classical curriculum. Our Catholic, classical approach: teaches the child how to think; follows the child's natural stages of learning; tailors the curriculum to the child; supports the spiritual formation of the child; allows the parents to play an integral role in their child's education; and provides counseling and tutorial support.

Contact information:
Fax: (805) 646-9921

Mailing Address
407 Bryant Circle
Suite B1
Ojai, CA 93023

Web address: www.motherofdivinegrace.org

RAINBOW RESOURCES

Mission statement: In business since 1989, it is our mission to provide the best educational products to homeschoolers, parents, and educators at the lowest prices we can offer. We currently carry over 40,000 quality educational products in all subject areas, for grades PK-12 and beyond!

Contact information:
Phone: 1-888-841-3456 or 800-705-8809

E-mail: info@rainbowresource.com

Mailing address:
655 Township Road 500E
Toulon, IL 61483

Web address: www.rainbowresource.com

132

APPENDIX B

SETON HOMESCHOOL
Mission statement: Nationally accredited by Southern Association Colleges and schools. Internationally accredited by AdvancED. The Mission of Seton Home Study School is to help parents fulfill their mission to educate their children for eternal salvation, as well as to be good citizens in this world to influence others to live the Christian life. Seton Home Study School exists because we are concerned about the education of Catholic children within their families. We are concerned that the education for Catholic children is truly Catholic. We are concerned that the rights and responsibilities of parents, as taught by the Church, are encouraged.

Contact information:
Phone: 540-636-2039. Toll free: 1-866-280-1930
Fax: 540-636-2648

E-mail: infopack@setonhome.org or admissions@setonhome.org

Web address: www.setonhome.org

SONLIGHT CURRICULUM
Mission statement: Sonlight Curriculum is a Christian homeschool curriculum company specializing in literature-based homeschool curriculum programs. We provide complete homeschool curriculum packages and individual resources and materials so you can build the preschool or K-12 homeschool curriculum that best meets your family's needs.

Contact information:
Phone: 303-730-6292

Mailing address:
8042 South Grant Way
Littleton, CO 80122-2705
Web address: www.sonlight-curriculum.com

133

5 STEPS TO SUCCESSFUL HOME SCHOOLING

THE WELL TRAINED MIND: A Guide to Classical Education at Home
A comprehensive guide to home education. This book will answer most questions you may have regarding home schooling. It outlines a complete education program for grades K-12. It lists curriculum and resources. A must have book for all home educators. Published by W.W. Norton & Company.

Web address: www.welltrainedmind.com

FAITH BASED PROGRAMS AND RESOURCES

THE BIBLE TIMELINE: The story of Salvation 24 Part Bible Study. By: Jeff Cavins. (Great for high school students, college and adults)

Web address: www.ascensionpress.com
or www.jeffcavins.com

CATHOLIC CHILDREN'S TREASURE BOX
These delightful books contain stories, poems, games, and things to make and do with pre-school and kindergarten age children. Many wonderful stories and activities to introduce young children to the Catholic faith.

Tan Books and Publishers, Inc.
Mailing address:
P.O. Box 424
Rockford, IL 61105

Web address: www.tanbooks.com

134

APPENDIX B

DESIGNING YOUR OWN CLASSICAL CURRICULUM: A Guide to Catholic Home Education. Third Edition. Berquist, Laura M. Ignatius Press. San Francisco. 1998.

FAITH AND LIFE SERIES
A catechetical program for grades one through eight. Published by Catholics United for the Faith, Inc. Steubenville, OH. 2008

Web address: www.faithandlifeseries.com
or www.ignatius.com

IGNATIUS PRESS
Ignatius Press offers a series of books about different saints. The books are written for children. We have found them to be captivating – a very interesting way to learn about the saints and our Catholic faith. Our favorite is *The Cure of Ars: The Priest Who Out-Talked the Devil by Milton Lomask.*

Web address: www.ignatius.com

LIGHTHOUSE CATHOLIC MEDIA CD'S (Excellent for high school, college and adults)

Contact information:
Phone: 866-526-2151

E-mail: CDClubinfo@LighthouseCatholicMedia.org

Web address: www.LighthouseCatholicMedia.org

PROVE IT! GOD. And other books in the Prove It! series by Amy Welborn (This is a great apologetics series written for middle school students). Published by Our Sunday Visitor Press.

Web address: www.amywelborn.com

5 STEPS TO SUCCESSFUL HOME SCHOOLING

ST. JOSEPH'S BALTIMORE CATECHISM. Bennet, Fr,. C.P.
Catholic Book Publishing Corp. New York. 1969-1962.

HISTORY PROGRAMS AND RESOURCES

AMERICA'S CATHOLIC HERITAGE
This textbook, along with other history resources from Seton Press
provides a thorough look at American history from the Catholic
perspective. Offers interesting information about the role Catholics
played in the founding of our nation.

> Phone: 540-636-2039. Toll free: 1-866-280-1930
> Fax: 540-636-2648

> E-mail: infopack@setonhome.org
> or admissions@setonhome.org

ABRAHAM LINCOLN and other books by Ingri and Edgar Parin
d'Aulaire. These beautiful biographies for children tell the stories
of famous people from history. Published by Beautiful Feet Books.

> Contact information:
> Phone: 800-889-1978

> Mailing address:
> 139 Main Street
> Sandwich, MA 02563

> Web address: www.bfbooks.com

BETHLEHEM BOOKS
Publishers of excellent books for children. *Galen and the Gateway
to Medicine*, and other books in this series are wonderful biographies
that offer an interesting way to learn about a historical person and the

136

APPENDIX B

time in history in which they lived.

Mailing address:
10194 Garfield Street South
Bathgate, ND 58216

Phone: 1-800-757-6831

Web address: www.bethlehembooks.com

HOW THE REFORMATION BEGAN
Written by Hilaire Belloc. Published by Tan Books and Publishers.
Excellent high school history text. Comprehensive, historical account
of the Reformation through the Catholic lens. Great for adults to read
too!

Web address: www.tanbooks.com

MOZART: THE WONDER BOY and other books in this series by
Opal Wheeler and Sybil Deucher. These wonderful biographies
for elementary students tell the story of classical composers in an
interesting and exciting way. Zeezok Publishing. Elyria, OH.

THE OLD WORLD AND AMERICA by Rev. Philip J. Furlong, Ph.D.
An excellent middle school history text. Recommended by Laura
Berquist. Published by Tan Books and Publishers, Inc.

Mailing address:
P.O. Box 424
Rockford, IL 61105

Web address: www.tanbooks.com

*THE STORY OF THE CHURCH: Her Founding, Mission, and
Progress. A Textbook in Church History.* Rev. George Johnson,
Ph.D., Rev. Jerome D. Hannan, Ph.D., J.C.D., and Sister M.

137

5 STEPS TO SUCCESSFUL HOME SCHOOLING

Dominica, O.S.U., Ph.D. Published by Tan Books and Publishers.

Web address: www.tanbooks.com

THE STORY OF THE WORLD
This history series is a complete, classical history program. It begins with Ancient Times and continues, through four volumes, to Modern Times. Written by Susan Wise Bauer. Peace Hill Press.

Contact information:
Phone: 1-877-322-3445
Fax: 804.829.5704

Mailing Address:
18021 The Glebe Lane
Charles City, VA 23030

Web address: www.welltrainedmind.com

THE ULTIMATE GEOGRAPHY AND TIMELINE GUIDE
A complete geography resource for grades K-12. Written by Maggie Hogan and Cindy Wiggins. Published by GeoCreations, Ltd.

Phone: 877-492-7879

Web address: www.geomatters.com

ENCYCLOPEDIA OF WORLD HISTORY. Internet Linked. Published by Usborne Books. Excellent history resource.

Web address: www.UsborneBooks.com

THE WORLD OF COLUMBUS AND SONS and other books by Genevieve Foster. Excellent historical books for middle school and high school students. Looks at what was happening throughout the world during the time of one historical character. Published by

138

APPENDIX B

Beautiful Feet Books. Sandwich, MA.

Contact information:
Phone: 800-889-1978

Mailing address:
139 Main Street
Sandwich, MA 02563

Web address: www.bfbooks.com

WHATEVER HAPPENED TO PENNY CANDY? And other books
by Richard J. Maybury in the "Uncle Eric" series. These books,
appropriate for high school age students, take a look at different
aspects of civics and government from economics to voting and
many areas in between. These practical books are not written from
a Catholic worldview, but may spark interesting and important
discussions between parents and their teens. Recommended to read
with your high school students.

Bluestocking Press

Web address: www.BlueStockingPress.com

LANGUAGE PROGRAMS AND RESOURCES

AMERICAN CARDINAL READERS
Originally created for Catholic Parochial Schools, these delightful
books contain short stories, many of a Catholic nature, at appropriate
reading levels. Each of the nine books advances in its level of
difficulty. Republished by The Neumann Press. Long Prairie, MN.

Web address: www.neumannpress.com/amcarreadset.html

139

DAYS GO BY SERIES

Beautiful Christian readers. These wholesome books, along with their accompanying workbook and teacher resource are a wonderful way to teach reading and grammar to the elementary student. Published by Pathway Publishers. LaGrange, IN.

Web address: www.pathwayreaders.com

ENGLISH FROM THE ROOTS UP

100 Greek and Latin roots used by students in grades 2-12 for understanding the fundamentals of English and building vocabulary. English From the Roots Up is also widely used to prepare for SATs.

Web address: www.cunepress.com

EXPLODE THE CODE

Simple work books and teacher guides that help earlier readers learn to read, write, and spell. Educators Publishing Service. Cambridge, Mass. Most home school suppliers sell these workbooks.

www.rainbowresource.com or www.explodethecode.com

GRAMMAR WORKS AND PHONICS PROGRAM

A complete grammar and reading program for elementary, middle school, and high school age students. Written by Jay W. Patterson. Published by Holly Hall Publications.

Mailing address:
25234 County Highway 55
Henning, MN 56551

Phone: 218-583-2826

Web address: www.theworkspeople.com

APPENDIX B

INSTITUTE FOR EXCELLENCE IN WRITING
An effective method for teaching writing skills, IEW offers writing programs for students in grade school through high school. This program is superior to every other program I have seen. It is comprehensive, offers excellent parent teacher resources, and teaches writing skills that surpass anything currently offered in most schools.

Phone: 800.856.5815   (local 918.894.5802)
Fax: 603.925.5123

Email: info@excellenceinwriting.com

Mailing address:
8799 N. 387 Rd.
Locust Grove, OK 74352

Web address: www.excellenceinwriting.com

LEARNING LANGUAGE ARTS THROUGH LITERATURE
This excellent language arts program is a fully integrated language arts program that teaches grammar, reading, spelling, vocabulary, writing mechanics, creative writing, thinking skills and more through the use of classic literature. Very user friendly program. Written by Susan Simpson and Debbie Strayer. Published by Common Sense Press.

Web address: www.commonsensepress.com

TEACH YOUR CHILD TO READ IN 100 EASY LESSONS
Written by Siegfried Englemann, Phyllis Haddox, and Elaine Bruner. Published by Simon and Schuster. New York. Excellent program for teaching any child to read. Allows the parent and child to work at their own pace. I have used this with four of our children. I have also recommended it to others (even those whose children attend school but need a little extra help with learning to read). Found at most major book retailers and home school resource providers.

Web address: www.timberdoodle.com
or www.rainbowresource.com

THE WRITING ROAD TO READING by Romalda Bishop Spalding.
Edited by Mary E. North, Ph.D. Published by HarperCollins
Publishers. Arguably the most comprehensive reading and writing
program available. Very comprehensive. Offered by most book
retailers and home school resource providers.

Web address: www.spalding.org

MATH PROGRAMS AND RESOURCES

MATH-U-SEE

Phone: 888-854-MATH

Mailing address:
Math-U-See
PO Box 8888
Lancaster, PA 17604

Web address: www.mathusee.com

RIGHT START MATH
Phone: 888-272-3291 or 701-782-2000
Fax: 701-782-2007

Mailing address:
Activities for Learning, Inc.
321 Hill Street
PO Box 468
Hazelton, ND 58544

APPENDIX B

E-mail: Info@ALabacus.com
Web address: www.alabacus.com

SAXON PUBLISHERS
Phone: 800-284-7019

Mailing address:
2600 John Saxon Blvd.
Norman, OK 73071

Web address: www.saxonpublishers.com

SINGAPORE MATH
Phone: Phone: 503-557-8100
Fax: 503-557-8103

Mailing address:
404 Beavercreek Road #225
Oregon City, OR 97045

Web address: www.singaporemath.com

VIDEO TEXT ALGEBRA
Phone: 1-800-ALGEBRA (1-800-254-3272)
Fax: 317-622-1396

E-mail: customercare@videotext.com

Web address: www.videotext.com

SCIENCE PROGRAMS AND RESOURCES

APOLOGIA EDUCATIONAL MINISTRIES
Apologia offers comprehensive science programs for middle school

5 STEPS TO SUCCESSFUL HOME SCHOOLING

and high school students. Their textbooks offer a thorough and extensive look at each category of science (astronomy, biology, general science, chemistry, etc.), in a user friendly product. Science is presented from a Christian worldview.

Phone: 888-524-4724

Mailing address:
1106 Meridian Plaza
Suite 220
Anderson, IN 46016

Web address: apologia.com

CHRISTIAN LIBERTY NATURE READER SERIES
This series is designed to improve elementary students' reading skills as well as "their understanding of and delight in God's wonderful creation." Published by Christian Liberty Press. Sold by many Christian homeschool resource providers.

Web address: www.christianlibertypress.com

JONATHAN PARK SERIES
A dramatic science radio series prepared by Vision Forum. Through the exciting, fictional stories of the characters, science is presented in a fun, easy to understand, and gripping format. Some of the products offered by Vision Forum are hostile toward the Catholic Church. These CD's, although they present a fundamental approach to Scripture, are not anti-Catholic. They present a Creationist view of science throughout their episodes.

Web address: www.visionforum.com

THE MAGIC SCHOOL BUS SERIES
Wonderful books for elementary students published by Scholastic Books. Although secular, and coming from an evolution perspective,

APPENDIX B

they offer a supplemental option to your science program.

Web address: www.scholastic.com/magicschoolbus

MOODY SCIENCE CLASSICS
Science presentations on DVD. Each 20 minute – 60 minute
video focuses on one area of science with a Christian world view.
Although these video presentations were produced many years ago,
what they lack in special effects and cinematography, they make up
for in easy to understand science lessons and demonstrations.

Web address: www.moodypublishers.com

USBORNE SCIENCE ENCYCLOPEDIA. Internet Linked.
Published by Usborne Books.

100 SCIENCE EXPERIMENTS published by Uborne Books

Web address: www.UsborneBooks.com

Appendix C

Sample Daily Home School Schedules

5 Steps to Successful Home Schooling

Sample Daily Schedule #1: Spreadsheet Format

	Child #1	Child #2	Child #3	Child #4	Child #5	Child #6
8:00						
8:30						
9:00						
9:30						
10:00						
10:30						
11:00						
11:30						
12:00						
12:30						
1:00						
1:30						
2:00						
2:30						
3:00						
3:30						
4:00						
4:30						
5:00						
evening						

APPENDIX C

SAMPLE DAILY SCHEDULE #2:
MODERATELY FLEXIBLE FORMAT

Between 8am and 10:30am Complete These Subjects/Tasks

1.

2.

3.

4.

5.

Between 10:30am and Noon Complete These Subjects/Tasks

1.

2.

3.

Between 1:00pm and 3:00pm Complete These Subjects/Tasks

1.

2.

3.

5 STEPS TO SUCCESSFUL HOME SCHOOLING

SAMPLE DAILY SCHEDULE #3: FLEXIBLE FORMAT (BEST FOR OLDER, MORE RESPONSIBLE STUDENTS)

Complete These Subjects and Their Outlined Assignments Today/ This Week

1.

2.

3.

4.

5.

6.

7.

8.

Complete These Tasks/Chores/Responsibilities Today

1.

2.

3.

4.

BIBLIOGRAPHY

Benedict's Way: An Ancient Monk's Insights for a Balanced Life. Pratt, Lonni Collins and Homan, Fr. Daniel OSB. Loyola Press. Chicago. 2000.

Catechism of the Catholic Church. Second Edition. Libreria Editrice Vaticana. 1994.

Catholic Homeschool Support. www.catholichomeschool.org

The Catholic Study Bible: New American Bible. Senior, Donald. Getty, Mary Ann. Stuhlmueller, Carroll. Collins, John J. Oxford University Press. New York. 1990.

A Christian's Prayer Book: Psalms, Poems and Prayers for the Church's Year. Coughlan, Peter; Jasper, Ronald C.D.; and Rodrigues, Teresa O.S.B. Franciscan Herald Press. Chicago.

5 STEPS TO SUCCESSFUL HOME SCHOOLING

Designing Your Own Classical Curriculum: A Guide to Catholic Home Education. Third Edition. Berquist, Laura M. Ignatius Press. San Francisco. 1998.

The Holy Rosary. Lovasik, Fr. Lawrence S.V.D. Catholic Book Publishing Company. New York. 1978

"Home Educating the Special Needs Child". (MACHE Handbook, Special Needs Section 2-3. Minnesota Association of Christian Home Educators. 2008.

Homilies for the Active Christian. Weber, Fr. Arnold O.S.B. Cabin Six Books. St. Paul, MN. 2006.

How to Pray the Rosary. Lighthouse Catholic Media. Streamwood, IL.

"How to Write a Mission Statement." Radtke, Janel M. Copyright 1998. The Grantsmanship Center. www.tgci.com.

"Introduction to Lectio Divina." Dysinger, Fr. Luke O.S.B. www.valyermo.com/ld-art.html. 2010.

"The Lost Tools of Learning." Sayers, Dorothy. Oxford. 1947.

"The Mass Explained." Richards, Fr. Larry. Lighthouse Catholic Media CD. 2010.

BIBLIOGRAPHY

"Mission Statement." Wikipedia. http://en.wikipedia.org/wiki/Mission_Statement. 2010.

A Mother's Rule of Life: How to Bring Order to Your Home and Peace to Your Soul. Pierlot, Holly. Sophia Institute Press. Manchester, New Hampshire. 2004.

St. Benedict's Rule for Monsteries. Translated by Doyle, Leonard J. The Liturgical Press. Collegeville, MN.

St. Therese of Lisieux: Story of a Soul. Study Edition. Foley, Marc O.C.D. and Clarke, John O.C.D. ICS Publications. Washington, D.C. 2005

"The Seven Habits of Highly Effective Families; Our Exclusive Interview with Dr. Stephen Covey." Kochenderfer, Rebecca. Homeschool.com. The #1 Homeschooling Community. www.homeschool.com/articles/Stephen_Covey. 2010.

So You're Thinking About Homeschooling: Fifteen Families Show How You Can Do It. Welchel, Lisa. Multnomah Publishers. Sisters, OR. 2003

The Well-Trained Mind: A Guide to Classical Education at Home. Bauer, Susan Wise and Wise, Jessie. W.W. Norton & Company. New York. 2004

"Why Do We Tell Children to Read?" Freedman-DeVito, Barbara. http://www.babybirdproductions.com. 2004.